STRATEGIC ORGANIZATIONAL CHANGE

Strategic Organizational Change

Building Change Capabilities in Your Organization

Ellen R. Auster

Krista K. Wylie

Michael S. Valente

palgrave
macmillan

First published 2005 by
PALGRAVE MACMILLAN
Houndmills, Basingstoke, Hampshire RG21 6XS and
175 Fifth Avenue, New York, N.Y. 10010
Companies and representatives throughout the world

PALGRAVE MACMILLAN is the global academic imprint of the Palgrave Macmillan division of St. Martin's Press, LLC and of Palgrave Macmillan Ltd. Macmillan® is a registered trademark in the United States, United Kingdom and other countries. Palgrave is a registered trademark in the European Union and other countries.

ISBN-13: 978–1–4039–9149–2
ISBN-10:   1–4039–9149–9

This book is printed on paper suitable for recycling and made from fully managed and sustained forest sources.

A catalogue record for this book is available from the British Library.

A catalog record for this book is available from the Library of Congress.

10   9   8   7   6   5   4   3   2   1
14 13 12 11 10 09 08 07 06 05

Printed and bound in China

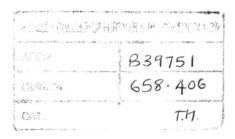

For change champions everywhere making a difference. Here's to you!

ERA, KKW, MSV

To my daughters Shannon and Lindsey, to my husband, Steve Weiss, and to my parents, Don and Nancy Auster.

Ellen R. Auster

To Emree and Madeline.

Krista K. Wylie

To all the children at the Hospital for Sick Children in Toronto; to my mother; and to all my friends and family.

Michael S. Valente

Contents

Contents

Figures

Tables

Acknowledgments

To my parents, Don and Nancy Auster, for your ongoing encouragement and support, for your sociological and economic lenses (both are retired academics), and for instilling in me the importance of compassion, being straightforward, trying to make the world a better place, and keeping life fun. Key ingredients for successful organizations – key ingredients for life.

To my daughters, Lindsey and Shannon, for your never-ending enthusiasm about my book writing and for keeping me laughing, centered, and making my life complete. You both are amazing – always optimistic, cheering me on, and making the most of our moments of celebration. Hugs and kisses to you both!

To my husband, Steve Weiss, for tolerating all my middle of the night note writing when I was percolating on an idea or chapter, for sharing the roller-coaster of writing this book, and for always believing I can do whatever I set my mind to.

You all inspire me, mean the world to me, and I love you all so very much.

I also want to thank the many students, executives, clients, colleagues, and friends who have molded my thinking on change. In particular, I am grateful to the Kellogg/Schulich EMBA KS01 and KS02 classes for their excitement and openness to testing out the ideas in this book and their terrific input and feedback. Ed Freeman and Jim Gillies also deserve special recognition for their upbeat and insightful advice at various key junctures. I am also indebted to Nadia Fahmy and Lisa Kay for their support and positive spin throughout the process, to Lisa Hillenbrand for all the learnings and fun with our P&G projects, and to Lynn Zimmer for knowing I could and should write this book.

Ellen R. Auster

A special thanks to Em for your unwavering belief in me, and your constant support and encouragement in all that I do. We have embarked upon many changes together and you have taught me plenty on the subject!

Thanks also to Madeline for being such a wonderful teacher. Every day I learn more about people, emotions, relationships, planning (and the importance of spontaneity too!) from you.

And finally, thank you to the colleagues and clients who have given me the opportunity both to lead change and to have change thrust upon me. These opportunities have lead to insights about change for which I am grateful.

Krista K. Wylie

I would like to express my thanks and admiration to Ellen Auster for her open mind, determination, and attention to detail. I would also like to thank the many researchers and authors that have influenced my thinking on this book. I am very grateful to the organizations for which I have consulted and worked with. Each organization offered a unique set of challenges that provided tremendous learning and experience that enriched the content of this book. I also thank the undergraduate students at the Schulich School of Business for their imagination, determination, and fresh outlook on business.

I would like to thank my mother, Delores Armieri, for her love and support, my grandfather Albert for making all this possible, Russell Zavitz and Angie Reid for their tolerance during the more challenging times of the book, my sister Tina for always being there, Alex for reminding me what it's like to be a kid again, and my good friend George.

Michael S. Valente

In addition to our individual acknowledgments, there are some shared acknowledgements that we'd like to express. We collectively thank Debbie Farrell for her excellent administrative support and Sonia Visconti for her energetic and proficient research assistance. We are also collectively indebted to the terrific team at Palgrave Macmillan for their commitment to our vision for this book and for making this publication process a pleasure. We gratefully acknowledge Stephen Rutt, Publishing Director, for his enthusiasm, contributions, and for turning this dream into a reality. Anna van Boxel, Assistant Editor at Palgrave Macmillan, and Sarah Lockwood at Curran Publishing Services deserve special thanks for their efficiency and skillful management of the publishing process.

Introduction

Companies in today's fast-paced and complex business environment must be flexible, innovative, and agile. While dynamism and change are vital for today's companies, leading change effectively is extremely difficult. In fact, more than two-thirds of change efforts fail. *Strategic Organizational Change: Building Change Capabilities in Your Organization* allows "change leaders" like you to overcome these odds and develop the long-run change capabilities needed to achieve ongoing success.

Many books on change fail to consider the multiple dimensions of change, the ongoing nature of any change process, and the larger strategic context within which change occurs. In addition, they tend to emphasize large-scale transformational change and speak primarily to top management. In contrast, *Strategic Organizational Change* enables you to cultivate the multiple capabilities required for ongoing strategic change – so that you are successful not only in this change initiative but also in the stream of future changes that will inevitably arise. It offers change leaders throughout your organization a comprehensive, multidimensional approach that can be applied to any type of change, or at any point in a change process. Covering all aspects of change from building commitment, leveraging what is already working well, and navigating the politics and emotions of change, to working through the implementation details, and inspiring ongoing learning, *Strategic Organizational Change* offers a unique value proposition that is unmatched in change books today.

Another important differentiator of this book is its practical, user-friendly, action-oriented approach. Tips, tools, and worksheets provided throughout the book ensure that you can immediately apply what you have read, move from concept to action, and customize the approach to your own organization.

This book is grounded in the strategic organizational change (SOC) framework, a systematic and multidimensional approach that provides you with a roadmap for cultivating change capabilities in your organization. More specifically, the framework drills down on nine different dimensions of change to address the three essential questions of any change: "Where are we now?", "What do we need to change?", and "How will we implement those changes and build in dynamism?"

Each chapter is devoted to understanding and working through one of the nine dimensions of the SOC framework. For example, the chapter on assessing the external context demonstrates how macro trends, competitors, customers, and other external stakeholders can be leveraged in change, and assists change leaders in building a compelling case for the need for change. The chapter on working through the politics of change gives change leaders tools for engaging the people that can mobilize change and for winning over potential resistors. The chapter on the emotions of change provides concrete tips for helping people navigate the emotional roller-coaster associated with change. The SOC framework, combined with each chapter, demystifies the nebulous journey of change by providing both insight and actionable tools to use throughout the change process.

This new and comprehensive approach integrates and extends leading change perspectives, making *Strategic Organizational Change* a powerful, unique, and indispensable resource. By giving you the tools to create an organization that is change-capable and set up for both short- and long-run success, you can ensure a bright and energetic future for your organization.

GETTING THE MOST OUT OF THIS BOOK

In each chapter, we have created helpful user-friendly design features to summarize key ideas, to provide examples, and to put ideas into action.

At a Glance
Crystallizes the key ideas, allows for quick understanding of the chapter, and facilitates the easy selection of topics that may be of most interest.

By definition
Makes sure everyone is on the same wavelength when change jargon is tossed around.

A case in point
Presents illustrative examples that bring concepts and ideas to life.

Ahead of the curve
Shares leading-edge ideas that will help ensure your change initiatives succeed.

Heads up
Offers a "heads up" so you can avoid common pitfalls experienced in change.

Key takeaways
Summarizes the key ideas and learnings from the chapter.

Tools
Provides user-friendly worksheets that enable specific aspects of the SOC framework to be put into action in the context of your organization.

1 Becoming a change-capable organization

It's not the strongest of the species that survives nor the most intelligent – but the one most responsive to change.

Charles Darwin

At a Glance
Becoming a Change-Capable Organization

- Change is everywhere
- Why most change efforts fail
- How do we beat these odds?
- What every change leader needs
- Using the strategic organizational change (SOC) framework

CHANGE IS EVERYWHERE

No matter what job title and company appears on our business cards, the ability to lead change successfully is a critical component of what we do. Increasing global competition, rapid technological advances, unpredictable economic forces, and demanding customers all mean that change is the rule rather than the exception in today's fast-paced business environment.

Our change challenges might include increasing customer responsiveness, expanding to new markets, integrating a recently acquired company, or improving product innovation. Regardless of the specific initiatives we are involved with, being an effective change leader requires finding an approach

By definition
Change leader: anyone in an organization working to make change happen. Change leaders achieve the desired results, energize the people around them, and lay the foundation for ongoing success.

By definition
Change capable: the ability to adapt and evolve successfully again and again, even though specific change initiatives may vary dramatically in terms of scope, depth, and complexity.

5

that allows us to both tackle the immediate change challenges presented and build the long-run change capabilities needed for ongoing success.

WHY MOST CHANGE EFFORTS FAIL

Despite the importance of being able to adapt and change frequently in today's turbulent business environment, two-thirds of change efforts fail. Some changes are wrong for an organization in the first place, and so never have a chance for true success. Other changes are exactly right for an organization but perhaps people within the organization aren't buying in, or the resources needed to make the change happen can't be secured. Politics and emotions, when ignored (as they often are), can also derail change. Or, maybe success is declared prematurely, causing a change to fizzle out. These are just some of the reasons that change efforts fall short of expectations.

> ## By definition
> *Strategic organizational change* leverages opportunities in the external business environment through changes in the internal workings of the organization. By considering multiple dimensions of the change process, change leaders become adept at understanding where they are now, what changes need to be made, and how they can implement those changes and build in ongoing adaptation and evolution.

Underlying this wide assortment of reasons for failure is the tendency to focus on a limited number of dimensions of change, to overlook the strategic aspect of change, and to view change as a one-time event that starts and stops. Organizations with these tendencies fail to cultivate the long-run change capabilities needed for ongoing success. They are unable to seize opportunities, leverage their core internal strengths, or sustain long-term competitive advantage, and will find themselves at a disadvantage to those organizations that are change-capable.

HOW DO WE BEAT THESE ODDS?

Although everyone would love to hear that beating these odds is easy, the truth is that change is complex and multifaceted. Therefore, we need an action-oriented and comprehensive approach that allows us to understand the complexity of change while providing a process that will lead to sustainable success. More specifically, we need an approach that continually enables us to:

- See the big picture and proactively address the key dynamics of our external context.
- Identify what is already working well and what the real problems are within our organization.

- Shape a future that addresses what needs to be changed now as well as what needs to happen to build long-run change capabilities.
- Ready the organization by making a compelling case for change and gaining the commitment needed to make changes happen.
- Navigate the politics of change by mobilizing those who are enthusiastic about the change and working with those who are more reticent.
- Recognize the emotional side of strategic change and provide the support needed to get folks on board.
- Address both the high-level plans and the specific details of implementation.
- Harness the creativity, knowledge, and spontaneity that can lead to unexpected yet amazing results, both now and in the future.
- Nurture change and enable the organization to continuously learn and evolve.

Ahead of the curve
The emphasis on each dimension is dependent on the change challenge.

Some changes may be rife with political issues and others may be emotionally charged. Indeed, each change challenge is unique and will require change leaders to emphasize each of the above dimensions to a greater or lesser degree. However, to become a truly change-capable organization, the ability to address all of these dimensions will need to be cultivated. Only then will our organizations be equipped to effectively and efficiently handle any type of change challenge.

Is there really an approach that can give me all this?

Many books overlook the importance of grounding change in a strategic context and tend to look at change as a discrete process that begins and ends. In addition, they typically emphasize large-scale transformational change accomplished predominantly by top management, and gloss over key aspects of change such as politics or emotions.

In contrast, we offer an alternative approach that is useful for any type of change, or at any point in a change process. We will help you and your team to work with all levels of your organization to nurture and culti-vate the multiple capabilities required

By definition
Your organization: throughout the book, the term "organization" is used to refer to the business unit that is relevant to you. If you are a small business owner, "your organization" might be the entire company. In a large company, "your organization" might refer to the entire company or your division or business unit.

7

for ongoing strategic change. Our approach will enable you to successfully tackle the change challenges you face now, and simultaneously build the change capabilities you need to successfully address the future changes that will undoubtedly emerge.

So the answer is yes! There really is an approach that can give us "all this." While it isn't as simple as some others we might have come across, using this unique approach to change will ensure we not only achieve our desired change results more quickly and easily but also develop the change capabilities necessary for long-term success.

WHAT EVERY CHANGE LEADER NEEDS

The foundation of our approach is the strategic organizational change (SOC) framework. See Figure 1.1, the SOC framework.

This framework ensures that we, as change leaders, can answer the three questions that are fundamental to change. These three questions are:

- *Where* are we now?
- *What* changes do we need to make?
- *How* are we going to implement these changes and build in dynamism?

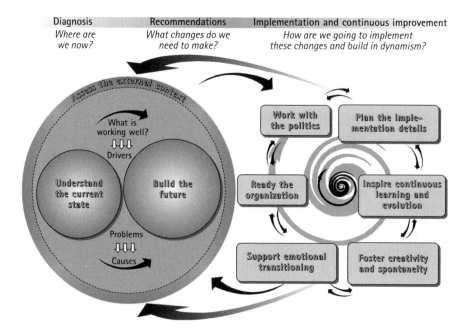

Figure 1.1 The strategic organizational change (SOC) framework

Where are we now?

Working from left to right in Figure 1.1, the first question posed in the SOC framework is "Where are we now?" To address this question, we need to assess the external business environment on an ongoing basis, and we need to understand the current state of our organization by identifying what is working well and uncovering key problems and their causes.

Assessing the external context. Taking the time to look at the broader context in which our organization does business is an integral part of answering the question, "Where are we now?" This might seem next to impossible with our packed calendars, and never-ending crises and meetings. However, ongoing external analyses provide valuable information about the political, economic, social, and technological context in which we operate, our competition, our customers, and other key external stakeholders. With this information, we can make sure the changes being pursued by our company are in line with the big picture, and we can build a compelling case as to why change is needed – something that is essential for gaining the commitment needed to make a change happen.

A case in point
Communicate external drivers for change

Our external analysis reveals that our largest competitor has recently introduced a new feature to their core software product, and as a result, won three of the last four deals our company was hoping to capture. Even though introducing the same new feature into our core software will take time, energy, and perseverance, we realize this is necessary to compete effectively. If everyone in our company understands the competitive pressures that are driving the move to introduce the new features, they are going to be more committed than if the change is introduced with no real explanation or context. Better yet, we can further cultivate commitment by involving those in our company in the process of deciding how to respond to this competitive threat.

Understanding the current state of our organization. Looking at the internal workings of our organization is the other integral part of answering the question "Where are we now?" This involves examining our organization in detail to pinpoint what is working well and also to identify the problems that currently exist and their root causes.

While most change approaches tend to only focus in on problems, identifying what is contributing to our current success is a critical aspect of change that is often overlooked. By understanding what is working well we can uncover what we don't want to tamper with during the change process, and we may also reveal processes or practices in our organization that it might be beneficial to replicate more broadly.

Heads up
Don't jeopardize what contributes to our current success

As part of our diagnosis, we want to ensure that any changes considered don't compromise our competitive strengths. For example, maybe our organization excels at rapid product innovation. While we might be pondering a change in organizational structure for other reasons, we would want to ensure that these changes do not undermine the rapid communication and decision-making capabilities responsible for our successful product innovations.

However, we also want to diagnose problems in our organization that need to be addressed and their root causes. We can uncover root causes by asking "Why does this problem exist?" To find the answer, we will need to analyze organizational dimensions such as strategy, leadership, structure, human resource practices, physical layout, technology, and culture. Usually this process requires digging deep and repeatedly asking "Why?"

A case in point
And the root cause is ...

Maybe our organization has lost 10 percent of its market share to our closest competitor. When asking ourselves "Why?", our first response might be to cite customer service as the cause. While that gives us some insights, we still need to dig deeper to find out "why" customer service isn't as effective as it could be. Maybe as part of that digging, we discover that a new bonus plan introduced earlier in the year rewards customer service reps for the number of calls they handle each day but doesn't seem to take into account the care with which they handle them. Perhaps, we also uncover that customer complaints are sitting in a database and aren't being directed to the folks who could remedy the issues they raise. So, in this case, digging deeper reveals root causes that may rest in the structure of the bonus plan for customer service reps and the lack of an effective process for taking action on customer complaints.

What changes do we need to make?

If we can answer the question "Where are we now?" then we are in a great position to move on to answering the question, "What changes do we need to make?"

The future of our organization. To be able to recommend the changes that not only solve the problems that exist within our organization but also position our organization for success, we need to be able to envision what our organization ought to look like in the future. From strategy to leadership to structure, each dimension of our organization can reveal an array of possible changes that it might make sense to pursue. Once a range of possible alternatives is developed, we can evaluate each possible change against specific criteria to develop an optimal path for change.

How are we going to implement these changes and build in dynamism?

The final question of the SOC framework is, "How are we going to implement these changes and build in dynamism?" as shown in Figure 1.1. When it comes to implementing changes, we need to do everything from ensuring we have the necessary resources and commitment, to navigating the political dynamics of our organizations. Specifically, we need to cultivate the ability to get ready for change, work with the politics of change, support people through the emotions of change, plan the details, foster creativity and spontaneity, and inspire continuous learning and evolution.

Getting ready for change. An important part of any successful implementation is taking the time to ensure our organization is ready for the changes that are being embarked upon. This means involvement, commitment, and understanding not only what the changes are but also why they are being undertaken. Readying the organization also involves securing the resources that will be needed throughout the change processes or finding creative ways to work with more limited resources. Without people's commitment and the necessary resources, getting through the inevitable highs and lows of strategic change will be more difficult.

Working with the politics of change. Different people in our organization will have different perspectives on change, depending on their perception of how a particular change impacts them. As people jockey to represent their interests, politics are likely to emerge. To ensure successful change, we need to be able to effectively work with these political dynamics. This means identifying influential people within our organization who are excited about change and tapping into their enthusiasm to propel change forward. It also involves identifying those key people within our organization who may be more

11

reticent about change and working with them to both understand their concerns and gain their commitment.

Supporting emotional transitioning. At the end of the day, change is about individual people transitioning to something new. Taking the time to consider how different individuals within our organization are actually feeling about a particular change is a critical part of any successful implementation. As change leaders, we need to be able to identify those folks within our organizations that are likely to say "You betcha" to change versus those that are likely to say "Not a chance." Only with this insight can we leverage those people who are open to change and help others work on their personal barriers to change, assisting them in transitioning towards the future more smoothly and quickly.

Planning the implementation details. The devil is, indeed, often in the details, and change can get derailed when these are overlooked. Things such as the pacing and timing of change, who will be responsible for key deliverables, how changes being implemented will impact customers, and what communication channels will be used are just a few of the types of details that must be considered to ensure successful implementation.

A case in point
A key detail: communicate with all key constituents

A large bank has been planning the implementation of a new online banking system for months. The switch to the new system is scheduled to happen over a weekend to minimize disruption to customers. However, the system will be unavailable to customers for a period of one hour early Sunday morning. Somehow, many bank customers are unaware of this one-hour downtime, and one of the displeased customers happens to be a reporter for a major news network. Before long, the bank's system reliability is questioned on the Sunday evening news. Oh, how a seemingly small oversight can jeopardize the long-term success of a change.

Fostering creativity and spontaneity. While it is important to ensure that important details don't get overlooked in strategic change, this doesn't mean that we have to plan everything and take care of every detail. Rather than trying to control entire change processes, effective change leaders find that letting folks run with various elements of change can spark and develop unexpectedly positive results. Furthermore, this type of approach helps build a passion for change that will be sustainable over time.

12

Inspiring continuous learning and evolution. Rapidly changing business environments imply that every change initiative will most likely be quickly followed by additional changes. To achieve sustainable success, organizations must not only navigate through a single change effectively, they must also build the ongoing capabilities required for continuous learning and evolution. Change-capable organizations inspire this continuous learning and evolution by continually engaging in ongoing external sensing, developing strong stakeholder feedback loops, leveraging collective knowledge, creating a change-capable context, and nurturing change-capable thinking.

Ahead of the curve
Be prepared for change

Even if we are not contemplating change, or in the midst of change right now, developing long-run change capabilities by helping folks become comfortable with the SOC framework is beneficial so that our organization is ready for change when it arises.

USING THE STRATEGIC ORGANIZATIONAL CHANGE (SOC) FRAMEWORK

OK, so now we have a sense of how each dimension of the SOC framework helps us answer at least one of the three key questions involved in change. Let's step back and think about how to best use this approach to change.

Use the whole thing

At first, the suggestion to go through each and every facet of a change might seem overwhelming. However, most people find that working through the entire SOC framework gives them the most insight and yields the best results. When beginning to use the framework, working from left to right – from diagnosis to recommendations and then to implementation – is the optimum route to take.

Diagnosing where our organization currently is enables us to make more informed recommendations about what changes need to be made. This diagnosis also equips us with the insight we need to understand how to make the changes happen.

Working through the question, "How are we going to implement these changes and build in dynamism?" ensures that elements such as politics, individual emotions, mobilization of resources, and planning details are not overlooked.

Ahead of the curve
Change is circular not linear

Although tackling the questions of change in a more linear fashion can serve us well some of the time, we may also find that in working through the question "How are we going to implement these changes?" we come upon excellent new ideas that should be incorporated into the change. For instance, we may find that in addressing the political dynamics of change and working with some of those people who are more hesitant about change in our organization, we discover new and insightful solutions for "what" changes need to be made. In cases like this, we should then circle back and revisit, "What changes need to be made?" before moving forward with the implementation.

Or, if emotions seem to be running high throughout our organization about a proposed change, focusing in on the reasons for those emotions may be a good place to direct our energies first. In short, if we think we can benefit from working through any of the portions of the framework earlier rather than later, then we should feel free to go ahead!

Customize the SOC as needed

The SOC framework offers a unique approach to change. It enables us both to see the complexity of change and to work through all the different facets necessary for achieving success not only for this change but also for the inevitable changes the future will bring.

How we use the SOC framework will depend on the specific situation and change challenges we face. Sometimes, we might work from left to right. Other times we might focus on particular aspects. And sometimes we might start with the "How?" and work back to the "What?" However we choose to use the framework, the process of using it will ensure we catch aspects of change that otherwise would have been missed. And, by catching those aspects, we will be more likely to beat the odds and become part of the one-third of changes that succeed.

Key takeaways for Chapter 1

- Use the SOC framework to build the capabilities required to beat the odds and achieve successful ongoing strategic change.
- Change-capable organizations excel at addressing these three questions:
  - "Where are we now?"
  - "What changes do we need to make?"
  - "How are we going to implement these changes and build in dynamism?"
- The SOC framework can be customized as needed for any specific change challenge.

2 Assessing the external context

We all know that the context in which our organization does business has many implications when it comes to change. In this chapter, we focus on assessing this external context, which is critical for diagnosing and developing our understanding of "Where are we now?" in the SOC framework. More specifically, as shown in Figure 2.1, this approach considers three main components:

- The macro forces in the business environment that impact our organization such as the latest social and political trends, economic forecasts, and technological advancements.
- The competitive landscape in which our organization operates, including direct competitors and indirect competitors, competitive dynamics, core competencies, and key differentiators.

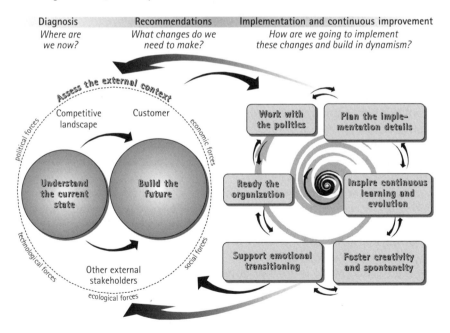

Figure 2.1 The SOC framework: assessing the external context

- Our customers, who can provide insights on strategic opportunities, and other key external stakeholders such as suppliers, labor unions, special interest groups, and trade associations that can provide ideas for change and opportunities for partnerships.

At a Glance
Assessing the External Context

- Looking outside the organization is critical
- Understanding macro forces
- Checking out the competition
- Don't forget the customer
- Leveraging other external stakeholders

LOOKING OUTSIDE THE ORGANIZATION IS CRITICAL

Jennifer, a fast-rising star within her company, implemented four successful changes within her division last year. These programs increased both sales and market share. When people in her organization talk about her, they say things like, "She always seems to be ahead of the curve" and "She seems to have a knack for knowing exactly what changes we should make in our organization to keep us competitive." Although Jennifer's days are packed with attending meetings and tending to crises that emerge, the importance she places on constantly assessing the big picture pays off not only for her but also for her company. As a senior manager within the Powertrain Group of a Tier 1 supplier in the automotive industry, she watches key competitors, conducts customer research on a regular basis, monitors economic and regulatory trends, cultivates good relationships with suppliers, attends conferences in her field, reads industry publications, tracks best practices, and keeps her eyes open for innovative ideas that can be used in her company.

While it can be easy to forget about what is going on outside our front door as we strive to keep up with our day-to-day responsibilities and determine what needs to be done inside our organizations, taking the time to step back and analyze what is going on in the external context of our business is essential. Doing so helps us determine what changes our organization ought to pursue both now and in the future. This process also helps us assess the viability of changes already in the works, and provides the justification needed to convince people that change is required. In the longer run, paying attention to these external dynamics and stakeholders enables our organizations to gain the understanding

18

and insights required to create a sustainable competitive advantage over time.

Ahead of the curve
When to devote extra attention to assessing the external context

Although assessing the external context is critical for all change-capable organizations, it is especially beneficial if:

- We are trying to figure out what strategic changes might be advantageous for our organization now and in the future.
- We are wondering whether a change already underway positions our organization well for the future.
- We are looking for ways to create commitment and a sense of urgency around a change.
- We are feeling that our organization tends to be too internally focused and misses key changes in the external business environment to which we should be attuned.

Calibrate strategic change with the external business environment

As change leaders, our external assessment enables us to get a view of the factors in the external business environment that impact upon our organization, and a deeper understanding of the context within which our organization does business. Using that assessment, we can see where our organization should be headed and what changes need to be made in order to get there. Understanding the external context is also vital for ensuring that any changes already underway make sense for the long-term viability of the company. Indeed, many companies find that staying competitive and attuned to their customers in today's fast-paced environment demands that ongoing change becomes a way of life.

Heads up
This isn't an event ... but an ongoing process

Regardless of the industry we are in, our organization will benefit from assessing the external context and building relationships with key external constituencies on an ongoing basis. Things in the external environment change all the time and if we only assess it once in a while, we run the risk of missing out on key information and getting surprised by trends and competitive moves.

Consider, for instance, a small company called Fresh that creates and markets 100 percent pure fresh juices through grocery stores in North America. Knowing that increasing consumer concern about health and pesticides has contributed to a 20+ percent annual increase in organic product sales in North America over the past five years, the marketing manager has proposed that Fresh introduce a line of certified organic juices. The social trends seem to indicate that the many changes needed to bring an organic line to market would be well worth the effort and costs involved. Introducing an organic line would also signal to customers that Fresh cares about the larger social issues around organic food. However, a broader scan of the business context might also reveal that a large competitor in the industry is about to launch its own line of organic fruit juices in grocery stores, and that the process for getting approval to market as "certified organic" is bureaucratic and potentially expensive. This additional information about the external context could modify the specific changes that Fresh embarks upon, or it might cause a reassessment of changes already underway.

Build the sense of urgency and commitment we need

Beyond ensuring that the changes being pursued are smart and strategic ones, assessing the external context provides the information we need to build a compelling business case for change. For people to feel committed to a change and be willing to move forward quickly, they need to understand the external realities behind it. As change leaders, we are in a great position to help build this commitment and urgency by sharing the key trends and competitive forces that are driving a change and by involving people in the process of assessing the external context. By taking steps such as these, we can easily convince people of the importance of change for the organization and the need to move forward with a change sooner rather than later.

Consider the management team at Fresh. They might decide to distribute the proposed organic line of juices not only to grocery stores but also to specialty health food stores and cafes in order to differentiate Fresh from

> **By definition**
>
> *Business case*: a persuasive argument that clearly articulates why a change is needed (or not needed) by outlining the positive (or negative) impact a change is expected to have on the organization and even the larger community. Generally, emphasis is placed on highlighting the short-run and long-run financial impact, although more and more organizations are now using a multidimensional bottom line for decision making. They consider how their business decisions can maximize value creation for all stakeholders, and think about the impact of their decisions not only on the organization, but also on society and the ecological environment.

20

the large competitor that is launching organic juices in only grocery stores. However, extending existing distribution channels will certainly impact those folks at Fresh responsible for establishing and maintaining new distribution relationships. Indeed, these people may be concerned that cultivating the required relationships will require extra time and effort, or they may be anxious about other implications of acquiring these new channels. Educating them about what is driving this strategic initiative is key. If they understand the strategic rationale for the changes and see that by extending their existing distribution channels Fresh will better position itself to succeed against its largest competitor, then some of their resistance to change could be avoided. Some people might also be willing to take on the additional work of cultivating new distribution relationships because the strategic shift towards organic juices aligns with their personal values.

Heads up
Creating urgency is harder than it looks

We want to be sure we don't fall into the trap of spending too little time on establishing a sufficient sense of urgency. It always seems to be more difficult than expected for people to let go of existing ways of doing things. In his 1995 *Harvard Business Review* (HBR) article entitled "Leading change," John P. Kotter noted that over 50 percent of companies he tracked had failed to create a sense of urgency for change. As a result, these organizations never gained the commitment required to even get a change initiative off the ground, never mind attain the desired results. One of the best ways to ensure our organizations *do* manage to create a sufficient sense of urgency is to share the external drivers of change.

UNDERSTANDING MACRO FORCES

There are an endless number of macro forces that can impact our organizations and almost as many frameworks for understanding them. One well-known framework that can help hone in on those macro forces most relevant to our organization is a PEST analysis. The PEST analysis considers four macro forces (**P**olitical, **E**conomic, **S**ocial, **T**echnological) that frequently impact organizations and the changes that they pursue.

It is easy to get caught up in the here and now when assessing the macro forces relevant to our organizations. However, every time we assess one of these external forces, we should not only understand its current impact but also anticipate and forecast how it is likely to change, and how those changes will affect our organization. Current trends can evolve over time and new trends can often emerge unexpectedly. In order to ensure that the changes we embark upon make sense not only in the short term but also in the long term, we need to take a long-sighted view of the macro forces that can affect our organizations.

While most notable trends and occurrences can be readily slotted into one of the four categories of the PEST analysis, we recommend including anything else of note going on in the external context, even if it doesn't seem to easily fit within this framework. For example, maybe a key resource needed for a product we're considering developing is endangered. While that might not be captured in the PEST, it might be valuable external information that could deter our organization from continuing this product development.

Ahead of the curve
Breaking out of our usual mindset can be a source of competitive advantage

With any scanning that we do, we should try to be aware of what factors we select out of the external context to focus on and how we interpret their impact. Our natural tendency is to focus on forces and elements that are in line with our way of thinking. However, our organizations might discover new sources of competitive advantage from noting the threats and opportunities that others miss because they fail to break out of their more limited mindsets.

Political

Political forces can refer to governmental regulations, legislation, political stability of governments, and in a broader sense can even include how activists and lobbyists might drive change in our organizations. For example, at the small juice company referred to earlier in this chapter, regulatory changes such as the introduction of new product labeling requirements by the Food and Drug Administration (FDA) would demand changes to the packaging of all the juice produced and marketed by Fresh. However, this regulatory change might be beneficial to Fresh, since a key differentiator of their product is its use of organic fruits.

If an organization is considering expanding to new geographic markets, either domestically or internationally, a careful analysis of political factors can be particularly important. A thoughtful political analysis will reveal both the new political opportunities and obstacles that crossing borders can involve.

Some examples of political factors we may want to continuously monitor when assessing the external context include:

- tax policies
- employment laws

- environmental regulations
- trade restrictions and tariffs
- political stability
- intellectual property protection
- favored trading partners
- anti-trust laws
- pricing regulations
- health and safety regulations.

Economic

Economic forces have far-reaching consequences for our organizations. For example, a recessionary period can severely limit the purchasing power of potential customers while a drop in interest rates might prompt a factory upgrade. In the case of Fresh, a strong dollar might restrict exports to other countries. As with political factors, our assessment should include the current economic conditions as well as a projection of future trends and their impact. Some specific economic factors we may want to continuously monitor when assessing the external context include:

- economic growth
- interest rates
- exchange rates
- inflation rates
- unemployment levels
- discretionary income
- infrastructure quality
- workforce skill levels
- labor costs
- business cycles.

Social

Social forces such as demographic and cultural factors can influence everything from the age distribution of the population, to consumer opinion, to the values that are driving market demand. For instance, in the Fresh example, the growing consumer concern about health and pesticides indicates a shift in consumer attitudes that will likely increase the market size for organic products, thus supporting the introduction of a new line of organic juices. The interesting question Fresh needs to grapple with is the longevity of this trend. In other words, is the shift towards eating healthier organic foods a fad or is this a social trend that is here to stay?

Some specific social factors we may want to continuously monitor when assessing the external context include:

- population growth rate
- age distribution
- social attitudes
- demographics
- class structure
- education
- culture
- leisure interests
- lifestyle changes
- birth and death rates
- values, norms, and customs
- psychographics.

Ahead of the curve
A positive contribution to society is also good for the organization

While assessing social forces, we may want to look for opportunities that might arise from aligning our company with social values or pursuing strategies that offer value to society as a whole. This might range from launching a major fundraising initiative in support of research and education on cancer, to offering products or services in developing countries to dramatically improve the living conditions or health and welfare of people around the world. For example, in 1987 Merck & Company began donating its drug Mectizan to tropical nations suffering from river blindness, a debilitating parasite-borne disease that infects millions of people annually. A decade and a half later, the impact is that millions of people have avoided infection and nation after nation has announced that the disease is no longer a major health threat. Initiatives such as these are worth pursuing. They clearly position our organizations as committed to larger societal issues. And beyond the obvious social benefits, such activities often yield tremendous visibility and media coverage, lucrative partnerships with other organizations, and increased employee and customer loyalty.

Technological

In today's business environment, technological forces impact upon virtually all organizations. Technology can dramatically transform an industry, can cut our new product development cycle time in half, or can mean that we must adopt certain technological capabilities to remain competitive. It is critical to not only stay on top of technological changes like these, but also anticipate how technology will evolve in the future, and how these changes might impact our organizations. Some specific technological factors we may want to continuously monitor when assessing the external context include:

- rate of technological change
- recent technological developments
- rate of technological diffusion
- new production processes
- scientific discoveries
- R&D activity
- level of automation
- government technology incentives.

Heads up
Fringe technology

We should always be on the lookout for technology on the fringe that has the potential to become mainstream and dramatically transform our industry. For example, most companies probably failed to anticipate the substantial role that both the Internet and email communication would have on their business.

Ahead of the curve
Add ecology too!

Many organizations are finding it beneficial to include an analysis of ecological forces and how their organization impacts the natural environment as part of their PEST, making the PEST a PEST(E). For example, a large Caribbean cruise company was involved in a scandal after its ships dumped toxic waste into harbors near their docking ports. Had the people at this company been paying attention to the ecological impact of their actions, they would have realized that not only would they be damaging their reputation in the short term, they would also be completely undermining the very thing that attracts tourists to take a cruise. Over the long run their behavior would both destroy these fragile ecosystems and destroy their ability to attract tourists at all.

In sum, having a good grasp on the external forces and dynamics going on in our industry is essential in today's fast-paced business environment.

PEST(E) trends can be key to organizations finding new and innovative ways to evolve both immediately and in the long run.

CHECKING OUT THE COMPETITION

Examining our competitors is another great source of information for figuring out what changes are needed within our organizations, how they might be implemented, and for assessing whether any changes already underway are appropriate. A first step is to determine which organizations we need to be watching. Many will be direct competitors but we might also find value in tracking companies that are indirect competitors. We will then want to drill down on the activities and performance of these companies to uncover what our organization can learn from them. Finally, we will want to compose a picture of what our specific industry looks like from a competitive perspective, and identify the critical success factors within our industry. We will also want to keep updating our view of competitors, and recognize that these dynamics continually change and evolve.

Heads up
Like a good chess player, anticipate the next move

Part of monitoring our external context on an ongoing basis includes considering how competitors will react and respond to what we do. Therefore, as we analyze our external context, we should focus not only on what is happening now but also on possible future scenarios of what the competitive landscape might look like given a series of actions and responses by players in the industry.

Who should we look at?

As a start, we should definitely consider our direct competitors. We may also want to consider those companies that our organization strives to emulate, or indirect competitors that offer substitutes for our product or service, and those "up and coming" organizations that might be on the periphery right now but could emerge as dominant players later on.

Direct competitors

Direct competitors are those companies that are in the same business as our organization. Of particular interest are those direct competitors that possess the largest or fastest growing share of the market. By looking at direct competitors, we will almost always uncover possible new ideas or paths that could lead to better results.

For instance, the juice company from the previous section would do well to check out the company that is launching a line of organic juices in grocery stores. They might find that this competitor uses in-store samples as a key advertising tool. Even though Fresh may have never considered this kind of labor-intensive promotional activity, the Fresh management team might see the positive results achieved by this larger competitor and consider experimenting with a similar approach in the health food stores and cafes it intends to use as distribution channels.

While we don't want to emulate our competitors all the time, considering what they are doing is important. We can then determine what makes the most sense for our organization, given our history, our strengths and capabilities, and how we are positioned in the industry.

Heads up
Direct competitors can sometimes appear out of thin air

We should be careful not to overlook those companies that operate within our industry but that are currently quite small and seemingly insignificant. While we may not consider these companies to be competitive threats at the moment, they certainly represent good learning opportunities and could easily grow to become more direct competitors. For example, some large software companies have experienced a significant loss in market share because they ignored the innovative potential of their small firm counterparts. Similarly, we should keep our eyes open for major players in other industries that may decide to diversify into our competitive arena, making them a new threat that we should track.

Indirect competitors

While direct competitors are usually quite obvious, we will also want to take the time to identify and track indirect competitors. Consider those organizations that provide products and services that consumers might consider as an alternate or substitute to those that our organization provides. These types of competitors can sometimes be tricky to spot since they can emerge from other industries. For example, the neighborhood bar that is considering major renovations would be well served by considering not only other bars in the neighborhood as competition (direct) but also the upscale coffee house down the street (indirect). Although the coffee house is in a slightly different industry than the bar, these two organizations compete for the same consumer dollars.

Drilling down on the activities and performance of competitors

Once we have identified which organizations make sense for us to track as competitors, we will want to consider their strengths and weaknesses and look at how well they are performing.

Strengths and weaknesses

We should start by spending some time analyzing our competitors with a critical eye. What are these company's strengths? Where do their weaknesses lie? As we assess their strengths and weaknesses, we will want to consider the activities of particular business units and functional areas. For example, a close look at our competitors' marketing strategies might trigger changes in our own product offering, pricing strategies, distribution channels, and promotional initiatives.

As we assess our competitors, we should also reflect not only on what they do but also on *how* they do things. Useful insights for our organizations might emerge in thinking about the processes that our various competitors use to do business. We might even want to pay attention to how they go about implementing change. Although not a typical aim of competitive analysis, useful insights about change implementation might be gained from considering both the successes and mistakes of competitors.

Performance metrics

In addition to our competitors' strengths and weaknesses, we will also want to look at their performance. We might examine traditional performance metrics such as market share, profitability trends, return on investment (ROI), and stock price. However, many companies take a broader and more comprehensive approach by taking into account not only a company's financial performance but also its positive and negative impact on the natural environment and society. This approach is often referred to as the "triple-bottom line." Other performance metrics we may want to consider include employee turnover, number of new patents, speed of product development, number of new products brought to market, customer satisfaction, employee turnover, or even the number of volunteers attracted and retained for a not-for-profit organization. Whatever metrics we use, we should use this data to enable us to see how our organization is performing relative to others.

Painting a picture of our overall competitive landscape

When we reflect on the overall competitive landscape, we should consider what is valuable, rare, and different about our organization. As well, we should identify critical success factors for our industry and map out the strategies of each of our direct competitors.

What is unique about our organization?

Understanding the capabilities and competencies that provide our organization's sustainable competitive advantage is critical for figuring out what we should and shouldn't change.

A common approach for assessing capabilities was championed by Jay Barney, author of *Gaining and Sustaining Competitive Advantage* (1997). He suggests that companies achieve sustainable competitive advantage when they possess capabilities that are *valuable, rare, inimitable,* and *non-substitutable.* In addition, he proposes that companies must have supporting processes and structures in place that enable these capabilities to be exploited. To apply this type of analysis, look at competitors in the industry and ask what they do that differentiates them from others. By carefully examining the differentiating resources or capabilities of our competitors, we can gain insight into the competitive dynamics of our industry.

By definition
Sustainable competitive advantage (SCA):
stems from unique and distinctive resources and/or capabilities that lead to superior performance over competitors. A competitive advantage is considered sustainable when competitors find it difficult to copy or substitute these resources or capabilities over long periods of time.

Critical success factors

Once we have assessed our competitors individually, we might want to step back and determine the critical success factors in our industry. What do companies need to do well in order to be successful in our industry given external trends and shifts? For instance, critical success factors in the fast food industry might include fast service, cleanliness, consistency and reliability in products, and a convenient, accessible location. By understanding these critical success factors, we can uncover the essentials our organization needs to keep apace with competitors. However, critical success factors may not provide us with the insights needed for achieving competitive advantage. In most cases, these elements are necessary to remain competitive in the industry but are not sufficient for competitive advantage. To gain competitive advantage, our organization needs to do something beyond these essentials to differentiate it and capture market share.

Creating positioning maps

Creating positioning maps of the overall competitive landscape in which our organization operates can be very insightful. Start by selecting some of the key components of strategy that all companies in our industry find critical. For instance, if our organization is a brewery, some key components of strategy within the brewing industry might be the international focus (that is, is each competitor selling in few countries or many countries?) and brand mix (that is, is each competitor carrying only a few brands or many brands?) Then, using two key components, map the competitors accordingly on a 2 × 2 matrix such as shown in Figure 2.2.

By constructing a 2 × 2 matrix in this fashion, we can gain insights into the strategies of key competitors and what types of strategic changes our company might consider to increase its success. Some of the best opportunities for competitive advantage emerge from what is not yet being done, so take note of the "white space" that emerges on the picture composed. In the example of the brewing industry above, there might be opportunity for a single brewer to be extremely successful by choosing a strategy that would place it in the top left quadrant – selling few brands in many countries. Be aware that white space can also be a warning that certain strategies are not worth pursuing. Returning to the example of the brewing industry, the bottom right quadrant might be an example of a strategy to avoid. Trying to sell many brands in only a few countries

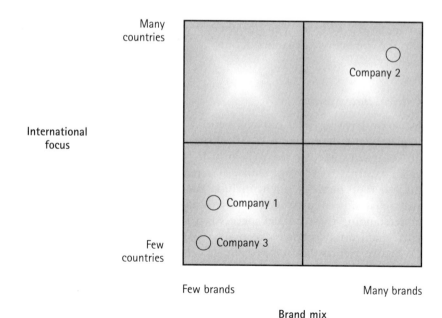

Figure 2.2 The strategic positioning map

30

might be difficult, and this might explain why none of our competitors are pursuing this strategy.

> ## Heads up
> *Competitive landscapes are complex*
>
> Keep in mind that the competitive landscape in which our organization operates is likely to be very complex. While these 2 × 2 matrices give a good perspective on untapped markets, recognize that they only capture a small slice of the competitive dynamics within an industry. In fact, to help compensate for this, we might want to make multiple maps that capture a number of key strategic elements of the industry.

Beyond our competitive landscape

Looking beyond our competitive landscape, we should consider organizations outside of our industry that have programs, products, or processes that are considered best in class. For example, even though our company might be in the mining industry, we might consider a company in the pharmaceutical industry that is known for its best-in-class environmental management program. This pharmaceutical company might have a number of initiatives that are leading-edge for managing the environmental impact of its products. By being open to looking out for best practices in other industries, our mining company can learn about new innovations that might not even exist yet in the mining industry. With a bit of creativity, we might be able to transfer these best-in-class ideas to gain competitive advantage.

We may also consider looking at companies that are succeeding within difficult industries. If a company is defying the odds and succeeding, despite the fact that its respective industry might be rife with negative conditions, then we can almost certainly learn something from it. For example, the store manager of an electronics store might take note of a small independent toy store that is thriving in an environment where other similar stores have been hit hard by the fact that more and more consumers are relying on mass-market stores and the Internet for purchasing toys. Learning *why* this toy store is succeeding could be a source of some good ideas for how our organization could evolve. For instance, maybe the reason this toy store is thriving is because it involves its existing customer base in focus groups in order to make effective purchasing decisions. Or, perhaps this toy store increases its number of visitors by holding regular special events that appeal to both children and their parents. Taking the learnings from an organization that is an exception to the rule in its own industry and transferring them to our own organizations can be valuable in generating the types of new ideas we need for ongoing change.

Consider the example of large retailers borrowing the concept of "ball and play" rooms from daycare centers. By taking a concept that worked well in one context and using it in a totally new context, these retailers have hit upon an excellent way for their customer service to evolve. What better way to encourage parents to shop (and buy!) than to entertain their children in a safe, supervised environment? Looking at organizations that are best in their class or doing something interesting even though they are outside our industry may add some rich insights to our assessment of the external context.

Heads up
Keep our eyes open for worst practices too!

Don't ignore the blunders that occur in other organizations. Since it is cheaper and less painful to learn from the mistakes of others, try to learn from organizations that have made mistakes or have the worst-in-class programs, products, or processes.

DON'T FORGET THE CUSTOMER

Staying keenly in tune with what our customers want now and what they may want in the future is a critical part of our external assessment, and may also uncover ideas about how our organization should evolve. By understanding how customers choose and use products or services, we gain valuable insights about the opportunities for change that exist within our industry. With this insight, we can discern the product and service attributes that draw customers to different competitors in our industry. We can also learn what customers are likely to value in the future.

There are a number of approaches for gaining information about customers in our industry. In this next section, we focus on some of these approaches to understanding our customers as part of the external assessment and as a key strategic driver of change.

Conduct quantitative market research

Large-scale quantitative research can offer useful insights about current customer usage, future trends, and changes in behavior or spending patterns. For instance, in an article entitled "The Myth of '18 to 34'" in *The New York Times Magazine* (2002, pp. 58–61), Jonathan Dee reported that organizations had, over the past four decades, spent the most money targeting 18–34 year olds whereas the baby boomers that accounted for half of all discretionary spending in North America had aged to become the 35–54 year old market segment. By failing to pay attention to what quantitative research reveals about demographic trends such as this, organizations can easily misdirect huge amounts of resources.

Try using focus groups

Consider running focus groups and speaking with not only customers but also frontline customer contact employees. This type of activity enables us to gain an in-depth understanding of customers in our industry and often is the catalyst for ideas on how we can differentiate ourselves from the competition.

Learn directly from customers

If we go where we can observe customers actually using the products or services we offer, we often find information we would never have collected otherwise. For instance, one organization that makes tools for use on construction sites found that the construction workers who used one of their products wore heavy-duty winter gloves to protect their hands – even in the heat of summer. When asked why, workers said that the tool was uncomfortable to hold otherwise. If this organization had relied on feedback from the purchasing department of the companies that bought their products rather than the actual users of their tools, they might never have discovered this weakness in the product. Instead, they were able to apply this knowledge about grips for tools to virtually every other tool they sold in the company. These types of direct customer insights can yield powerful ideas about important differentiators that can set us apart from the competition.

Another rich source of information that is often neglected is dissatisfied customers. Many organizations provide an opportunity to complain or return products. However, many fail to examine those customer complaints and use the information to figure out how to gain competitive advantage.

Although we tend to focus on customers we want or already have, valuable insights for future change can be gained from customers who no longer use our products or services. Unfortunately, once a customer leaves, they never again show up on customer satisfaction surveys. So, it's important to go after this group to find out why they were unhappy enough to abandon our product or service, why another organization's product or services looked better, and, ideally, what changes might be made to attract them back.

Ask those on the cutting edge

They might not be customers yet, but those people who are on the "cutting edge" and considered to be trendsetters can provide valuable information about future trends that are important for sustaining competitive advantage over the long run. For example, one large running-shoe manufacturer routinely goes to "teen hangout spots" in urban areas and gives away free shoes in exchange for ideas on how its shoes might be improved, as well as insights on future trends.

LEVERAGING OTHER EXTERNAL STAKEHOLDERS

Another aspect of assessing the external context, beyond the PEST, competitive landscape, and customer, is an examination of other external stakeholders pertinent to our organization.

As part of our assessment of the external context, we should also look at forces, trends, and potential future developments within these stakeholder groups. For instance, suppliers for Fresh might have had an unusually harsh winter that will likely affect the volume and quality of citrus fruits available. Or, maybe some of the company's key distributors have been experiencing difficulties with labor relations. Part of the external assessment for change leaders at Fresh would be to understand all of these players, the forces impacting their operations, and the implications as Fresh moves into the future.

Another critical source of competitive advantage can lie in our organization's ability to build and leverage relationships with these other external stakeholders. "Social capital" refers to the formal and informal connections that organizations have with their stakeholders. The value of these connections is the ongoing feedback they provide on key issues in the external business environment as well as the opportunity to build beneficial partnerships. In the longer run, analyzing social capital is essential because this process forces the organization to recognize that it is embedded in a network of interconnections with stakeholders. Failure to recognize those interconnections can result in missed opportunities ranging from good ideas to whole new market possibilities. For example, Fresh, the juice company we have been referring to throughout this chapter, could leverage its connections with advocacy groups for organic foods and find a win–win opportunity to put Fresh products in the vending machines in public schools. In contrast, lack of effective management of social capital can lead to situations where our organization gets blindsided by the unexpected actions of stakeholder groups.

> **By definition**
> *Stakeholders:* a stakeholder is defined as an individual, group, or organization that influences or is influenced by an organization. Examples may include customers, suppliers, distributors, business partners, investors, creditors, local communities, government, and employees.

Key takeaways for Chapter 2

■ Understanding the context within which our business operates can help us determine what strategic changes might be advantageous for our organization now and in the future, and can also help us in assessing whether changes already underway position our organization well for the future.

■ Raising awareness about competitive threats and external business realities can be key in creating commitment and a sense of urgency around a change.

■ As we work to understand the external context of our organization, we should make sure that we consider political, economic, social, technological, ecological, and other relevant macro forces.

■ Checking out the competition involves looking at direct and indirect competitors. Once we have identified those competitors, we should understand their strategies and drill down on their strengths, weaknesses, and their potential impact on our organization.

■ Identifying key differentiators amongst competitors, critical success factors, and using strategic positioning maps can help paint a picture of our overall competitive landscape.

■ For additional insights on sources of competitive advantage, we should look to organizations outside our industry that are considered best in class or are exceptions to the rule.

■ Many organizations overlook customers when assessing the external business context. Using quantitative market research, focus groups, and direct customer information often provides valuable insights for how our organizations can effectively stay ahead of the curve.

■ Leveraging stakeholder networks is critical for gaining access to new, realtime information about the external context and for building relationships that may enhance sustainable competitive advantage.

Tools
Assessing the external context tool

PEST(E)

Step 1: For each dimension of the PEST(E), identify key macro forces and their implications for our organization both now and in the future.

Macro force	Dimensions to consider	Which dimensions are key in our industry? What are their implications both now and in the future?
Political	For example, tax policy, employment laws, environmental regulations, trade restrictions and tariffs, political stability, risk of military invasion, intellectual property protection, favored trading partners, anti-trust laws, pricing regulations, health and safety regulations, etc.	
Economic	For example, economic growth, interest rates, exchange rates, inflation rates, unemployment levels, discretionary income, infrastructure quality, skill level of workforce, labor costs, business cycle stage (e.g., prosperity, recession, recovery)	*In our community,*
Social	For example, population growth rate, age distribution, social attitudes (health, environmental consciousness, career, etc.), demographics, class structure, education, culture (gender roles, etc.), leisure interests, lifestyle changes, birth and death rates, values/norms/customs	
Technological	For example, rate of technological change, recent technological developments, rate of technological diffusion, new production processes, scientific discoveries, R&D activity, level of automation, government technology incentives	*Projected T.V Recent bills, No cold calls, leaflets,*
Ecological	For example, implications and impact on the community, environment, natural resources.	*? ? ?*

36

Macro force	Dimensions to consider	Which dimensions are key in our industry? What are their implications both now and in the future?
Other key forces and external stakeholders	For example, suppliers, distributors, lobby groups, unions, government, community, etc.	

Competitive landscape

Step 2a: List our main competitors across the top row of the grid below. Describe their strategy and then assess the strengths and weaknesses of each main competitor in relation to our organization.

Step 2b: Note the potential impact of any indirect competitors and list other key insights about the competitive landscape of our organization (key differentiators, industry success factors, etc.) that it may be helpful to pay attention to when understanding our competitive positioning.

	Competitors			Potential impact of indirect competitors	Other insights about the landscape (key differentiators, industry success factors, indirect competitors, etc.)
	#1	#2	#3		
Strategy					
Strengths					
Weaknesses					

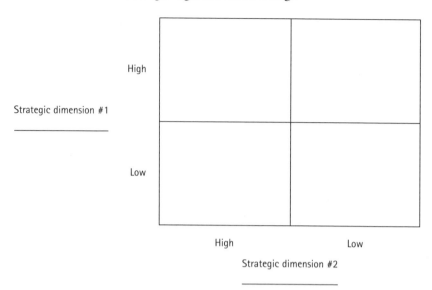

Step 2c: Try positioning maps

Start by identifying two critical strategic dimensions in our industry. Use them as labels along the horizontal and vertical axes. With an "X," identify existing direct and indirect competitors based on their positioning along these two dimensions. Circle areas for opportunity based on the white space or from areas where a competitor exists but experiences weaknesses that our organization can overcome. Repeat this process with additional relevant strategic dimensions in our industry.

Customers

Step 3: Note the methods our company uses to understand customers and what the key learnings are.

Dimension	Methods for understanding customers	Key learnings
Customers	For example, quantitative marketing research, focus groups, direct customer observation, and feedback, etc.	

So what?

Consider our analysis of macro forces, the competitive landscape, and customers done in Steps 1, 2, and 3 and answer the questions in Step 4.

Step 4: If this analysis is being used to assess a change about to be embarked upon or one already in progress, answer the following:

1. How does this external assessment support or not support this change initiative – both in the short term and long term?

2. What risks emerge from this external assessment that our organization needs to be aware of when pursuing this change initiative? Does the external assessment reveal opportunities that should be leveraged as part of this change initiative?

3. How can we use the information in this external assessment to make a convincing case for the need for change?

OR
Step 4: If this analysis is being used to determine possible change initiatives for the future, answer the following questions:

1. Given this external assessment, what opportunities exist for our organization and how can these be leveraged?

2. Given this external assessment, what threats exist for our organization and how can these be mitigated?

3. How can this external assessment be used to make a convincing case for the need for change?

3   Understanding the current state of our organization

In Chapter 2, we looked at assessing the external context in which our organization does business. To get a complete answer to the question in the *SOC framework*, "Where are we now?", it is also important to understand the current state of our organization. Although the current state represents a snapshot in time – since our organization is constantly evolving – it is important to stop and take this detailed look at "Where are we now?" to identify what is working well and key drivers, problems and root causes.

Without this type of analysis, we run three risks. First, well-intended change initiatives may undermine what is working well. Second, we may overlook key problems that explain our current situation. Third, we may not uncover the root causes of the problems we do identify and as a result never find effective solutions. In all of these cases, we will end up making changes that lead to less than optimal results.

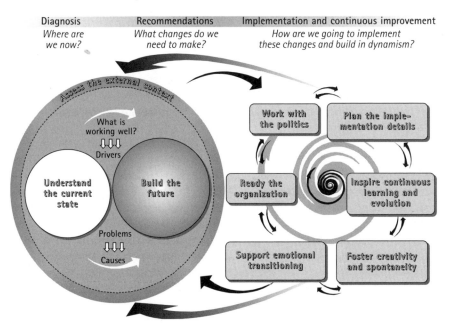

Figure 3.1 The SOC framework: understanding the current state

41

At a Glance
Understanding the Current State

- What is working well?
- Figuring out key problems
- Understanding the internal workings of our organization
- Peeling back the layers of the onion to determine key drivers and root causes

Ahead of the curve
When to devote extra attention to understanding the current state

Although understanding the current state is critical for all change-capable organizations, it is especially beneficial if:

- Our organization's performance has been suffering and we need to effectively address the problems underlying this poor performance.
- Our organization is quite successful but we are not sure what drives that success or how we can further leverage it.
- We are sure that there are internal practices that are not widely known or shared that our organization can learn from.
- We are wondering whether a change already underway is going to contribute positively to our organization.
- We are disappointed at the net results of a recent change and suspect that the change didn't address the real issues.
- We have identified changes in the external context of our organization, and are wondering how our organization can leverage this new environment.

There are many different ways that we can go about understanding the current state of our organization. We may be tempted to rely exclusively on our personal knowledge of the organization for efficiency purposes, but that may not give us all the information we need. Therefore, we also need to look to others in the organization to broaden our view. Some approaches that may be useful to gain a more comprehensive picture of the internal workings of our organizations include employee surveys, informal focus groups, and chats at the water cooler. Views from external stakeholders such as suppliers, customers, and even competitors can also offer tremendous insights. How extensively we collect information will likely depend on the specific change challenge we face and how well informed we are about the current state. As we go about collecting information, we will undoubtedly receive questions about what we are doing and why. To respond to those questions, we will want to find a balance between being transparent and prematurely raising unachievable expectations and unnecessary anxieties.

WHAT IS WORKING WELL?

Problems have a way of demanding our attention. However, there is also a lot of value in taking the time to identify what is currently working well within our organizations. This process can reveal the elements of our organization that we should not tamper with since they are contributing to its success. The process of identifying what is working well can also provide us with insight into what we can further harness to sustain competitive advantage.

Core capabilities and sustainable competitive advantage (SCA)

Identifying our core capabilities is often a good starting point when trying to discern our organization's competitive advantage. Core capabilities are combinations of resources, processes, skills, and know-how that define an organization's value proposition to its customers. Take, for example, a chain of retail stores called Tween that is focused on selling clothing for girls between the ages of 8 and 12. Core capabilities for Tween might include friendly yet hip customer service, established retail locations, and a store layout that makes shopping fun, comfortable, and cool for the target market it wants to attract, as well as highly functional for a large in-store inventory. In addition, Tween may be the only clothing retail chain that has built a long-term relationship with one of the largest entertainment giants in the movie industry.

By definition

Appreciative inquiry: the process of focusing on what is working well in our organization by identifying both core competencies and internal best practices is grounded in what is known as an appreciative inquiry approach. See, for example, Diana Whitney and Amanda Trosten-Bloom's recent book, *The Power of Appreciative Inquiry* (2003). Although most folks who focus on appreciative inquiry don't bridge into strategy and don't blend the appreciative inquiry approach with a root cause analysis, the power of appreciative inquiry stems from discovering positive aspects of the organization and working to protect them throughout the change process, and possibly even amplify and diffuse them throughout the organization.

43

Core capabilities such as these give us insight into what our organization does well, and are important to keep in mind as we work through our internal analysis and begin to think about the future. However, we should bear in mind that not all core capabilities are sources of sustainable competitive advantage (SCA). We will find that some core capabilities are simply necessary to survive in a given industry by keeping us at par with competitors. But there are also capabilities that act as key differentiators, enabling our organization to consistently outperform competitors. These are considered sources of SCA. Sources of SCA that can give an organization superior performance, as we may recall from Chapter 2, must be valuable, rare, costly to imitate, and non-substitutable. In identifying these, consider the following questions:

- How do we deliver unique value to the customer?
- What is unusual or rare about what we have or do?
- What is hard to imitate about us?
- What do we offer that our customers will have difficulty finding a reasonable substitute for?

For instance, friendly yet hip customer service at Tween is considered by many to be a valuable capability in the retail industry. But it certainly is not rare, inimitable, or non-substitutable. There is no doubt that with sufficient training, Tween's competitors can build an identical capability. So although this level of customer service is a core capability at Tween, it is not a source of SCA. On the other hand, Tween's unique ability to capture exclusive contracts with top teen movie stars is most likely an activity that is valuable, rare, and difficult to imitate and substitute.

So, it is useful to not only identify our firm's core capabilities but also to segregate those capabilities into those that are sources of SCA and those that simply keep us at par with our competitors.

A tool we have developed to help visualize this difference is the sustainable competitive advantage core capabilities (SCACC) matrix as shown in Figure 3.2.

The SCACC matrix is two-dimensional with core capabilities along the horizontal axis and SCA along the vertical axis. Each axis is separated by "yes/no" quadrants. As part of drilling down on what is working well, it is important to focus on the left side of the matrix. The other quadrants will be discussed in Building the future of our organization (Chapter 4).

The upper left corner of the matrix encompasses those capabilities that our organization does well and that also act as sources of SCA. Core capabilities that map onto this quadrant are some of the most important elements of our organization's success, and are critical to keep in mind as we work through our understanding of the current state.

The bottom left corner of the matrix is also important to focus on

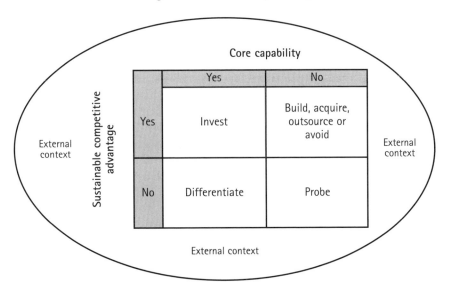

Figure 3.2 The sustainable competitive advantage core capabilities (SCACC) matrix

when trying to understand our current state. Core capabilities mapped onto this quadrant are activities that our organization does well but that are not sources of SCA. They are good practices that help the success of our organizations but they also run the risk of being easily replicated.

By referring to the external assessment and competitive analysis and revisiting the strategic implications worksheet from Chapter 2, we should be able to gain a pretty good understanding of what our organization does well in comparison to its competitors – our sources of SCA. We want to ensure that the changes we are considering don't disrupt these sources of SCA. We may also want to consider how to further leverage these sources of SCA as we move into the future.

Ahead of the curve
Let our customers help us identify our SCA

All the information we collected about our customers through the many different methods discussed in Chapter 2 also provide us with great insight about what our organization does well. Our customers give us direct feedback on what they like and dislike, along with how we can improve or what we can do more of to further our organization's success.

FIGURING OUT KEY PROBLEMS

While looking at our organization with a view to finding the positive is very valuable, it is equally important to figure out the key problems. Off the top of our heads, we could probably come up with a sizeable list of problems in our organization. Although this is a good place to start, it is also helpful to conduct a more systematic identification of problems by considering those that exist at the firm level, the group level, the individual level, and from the customer's standpoint. This type of approach forces us to consider not only the problems that directly affect us but also those that may be limiting our organization's success even though they are off our own personal radar screen.

Ahead of the curve
Don't forget to ask others

One way to get a good handle on problems at different levels is to seek feedback from others within our organization. Obtaining different perspectives on what is working and what is not working in our organization often yields insights we might have otherwise missed. This information can be collected informally through casual conversations, or more formally, through interviews or anonymous questionnaires.

Ahead of the curve
Define our scope

The scope of our current state analysis may vary, depending both on our organization and our role within it. For example, in a large company, we might restrict our analysis to examining only the internal workings of our specific business unit. On the other hand, for a project manager or a regional manager who interacts across multiple units, the current state analysis is likely to be more comprehensive.

Firm-level problems

Firm-level problems tend to focus on financial and competitive performance. Returning to the Tween example, firm-level problems at this organization might include declining sales, decreasing profits, and a loss of market share. However, as we work to identify problems in our organization, we should not restrict our analysis to considering only those problems that are easily identifiable. Instead, we want to think proactively

46

and take into account the long-term consequences of continuing to conduct business as we currently do. For example, although significant firm-level problems such as lack of new product innovation may not be as obvious as declining sales, their long-term negative impact on firm performance can be equally potent. Or, perhaps we want to build a stronger set of values in our organization. Thinking about how our company can truly make a difference could spark a reframing of what our organization currently does, and uncover a whole host of problems that need to be addressed.

Group-level problems

Group-level problems zero in on the dynamics between groups and within groups. For example, at Tween, there might be infighting between functional groups. Maybe there is conflict between the stores, the corporate marketing department, and the buyers. The stores may be frustrated that the buyers frequently miss the mark on the popularity of certain clothing items, and purchase either too many or too few items relative to customer demand. Similarly, the buyers may be frustrated because the marketing folks are frequently unable to provide the information that would enable the buyers to make smart purchasing decisions. At Tween, there may also be tension between stores because managers may not share ideas and information with each other, fearing that helping another store manager boost sales will make their own store look bad. These are all examples of group-level problems.

Individual-level problems

At the individual level, the focus is on the employees of the organization. Looking at Tween, some individual-level problems that might be present include absenteeism throughout the company and high turnover of store managers. Other examples of individual-level problems include lack of innovative ideas, low morale, stress and burnout, and poor work–life balance.

From the customer's point of view

Taking the point of view of our customers can also be very informative when trying to get a complete picture of the key problems in our organization. In Chapter 2, the customer was considered as part of the assessment of the external business environment. In this chapter, the customer is considered as a potential source of information about the problems that exist within our organization. For example, at Tween, customer interviews at a sampling of the stores might reveal that many customers are frustrated with slow checkout lines and have the impression that many of the clothes are not as trendy as they had hoped. In addition, analyses of customer profiles may indicate that most of Tween shoppers are 13 to 15 years old and that Tween is performing poorly in attracting the 8 to 12 year old target market.

Heads up
Be specific

As we are identifying problems in our organization, we want to be as specific as possible in articulating them. For example, rather than stating that the problem is poor customer service, we should try to define the problem more specifically. Perhaps the problem is too few salespeople for the number of customers, or inadequate training for salespeople, or a limited inventory. By defining the problem more specifically, finding the root cause of these problems will be easier and our chances of actually resolving the problems will be increased.

Ahead of the curve
Try reframing a problem

By framing problems positively rather than negatively, we can create a more receptive atmosphere for change. For example, if the problem is slow product development, it could be reframed as, "How can we improve the speed of time to market?"

UNDERSTANDING THE INTERNAL WORKINGS OF OUR ORGANIZATION

Once we have a good idea of what is working within our organization and what isn't, we then need to take a detailed look at the internal workings of our organization to complete our understanding of the current state. This detailed look at internal workings will help us to better understand the *key drivers* behind what is working well. It will also help us uncover the *root causes* of the problems we have identified. Only by understanding the key drivers behind what is working well and the root causes of problems will we be able to effectively determine the changes required in our organization.

A good way to get a handle on the internal dynamics of our organization is to analyze the following eight dimensions of the SOC wheel depicted in Figure 3.3 around "Understand the current state" and their interrelationships with each other:

Figure 3.3 The SOC wheel

Ahead of the curve
The value of multiple points of view

As we work to understand the current state, we should try to step into the shoes of others in our organization so that our analysis reflects many different vantage points. Some of the different angles we might take a look from include:

- top management
- middle management
- different divisions and functions within the organization
- frontline employees
- customers.

Strategy

When taking a look at our organization's current state, we can consider two aspects of strategy: competitive positioning and strategic objectives. Competitive positioning refers to which products or services our organization offers to which markets, relative to its competitors. Even more importantly, competitive positioning refers to how our organization derives a sustainable advantage over its competitors. Both the positioning map discussed in Chapter 2 and the SCACC matrix presented earlier in this chapter provide great visual representations of this aspect of strategy. Strategic objectives are the more tactical aspect of strategy, and refer to the specific goals or targets an organization must attain to ensure it is successful in realizing its strategy and competitive positioning. Strategic objectives can be set for any unit within the organization, and generally state what is to be accomplished by when. For example, at Tween, strategic objectives for the entire company might include an 8 percent growth in annual revenues and a 5 percent annual increase in the donations the company makes to children's hospitals. A strategic objective for one store might be 10 percent growth in annual sales.

While not every organization is able to clearly articulate its strategy, rest assured that all organizations have one. It is critical to understand the current strategy of our organizations because it provides the anchor for the internal operations. Everything that goes on inside our organization should support and reinforce our organization's strategy. If it does, then this might be a clue as to a key driver behind what is working well. If it doesn't, then this might be a clue as to some of the causes behind an organization's problems.

Leadership

Leadership is the process of creating a vision and moving an organization towards realizing this vision. To understand our current state, we need to take a look at the people who play leadership roles throughout our organization and how they work with their teams and units to meet strategic objectives and develop a vision of the future. This analysis gives us insight into how and why our organization runs the way it does, and can reveal both drivers of strengths and causes of specific problems.

For example, the regional managers at Tween should understand the leadership within each of the stores for which they are responsible – particularly those stores that are excelling and those that are having problems. By examining the leadership approach of the manager at one of the stores that consistently falls short of its sales targets, a regional manager might find that one of the reasons behind these poor sales figures is the store manager's inability to communicate the company's vision and the store objectives to employees.

> ## By definition
> *Vision*: a picture of the future of our organization. While different people can articulate their vision in different ways, vision usually refers to where the organization should head and how the organization should look in the future. A vision might also include key values that provide a strong moral foundation for the organization. Strong values articulated within a vision for an organization can be a powerful source of passion, enthusiasm, and strength in any change process.

> ## Heads up
> *Look beyond the title*
>
> As we think about the leadership within our organization, we should remember to look beyond people's titles. Leaders aren't only those people with impressive titles. Sometimes within a change process, people such as administrative assistants or line supervisors play important informal leadership roles in the organization. Considering the role of these people can be just as important as considering the vice-president's role for understanding the organization.

With this understanding of the store manager's leadership, the regional manager is in a better position to make changes that will solve the problems identified.

Structure and process

"Structure" refers to the basic form or architecture of an organization. From the structure flow the many processes that enable the various business units within an organization to come together. Both the structure of an organization and the processes that flow from it can impact success. Understanding this basic architecture can give us insight into the key drivers of what is working well, and the causes of problems.

A good starting point for getting a handle on our organization's structure is to consider the number of levels that exist. Some organizations are very flat whereas other organizations have many layers and levels. For example, at most companies, divisions such as R&D are quite flat whereas sales divisions may have a number of levels.

In addition to a scan of the number of levels that exist, consider how all the levels actually fit together in the organization chart. Usually, we find that some aspects of our organization's structure are based on function, others on product or service, and others on geographic region. Each type of structure has a number of pros and cons that are important to consider. By focusing in on the advantages and disadvantages of different types of structure for different units and levels in our organization, we can uncover both key drivers and root causes. See Table 3.1 for an overview of different types of organization structures and their advantages and disadvantages.

For example, the problem that one organization has in meeting its customer needs might stem in part from a functional structure where marketing is isolated from research and development, which makes communication and coordination difficult. In product structures, common problems are duplication, redundancy, inefficiency, and underutilization of resources since groups often don't share well with each other. So if there is a product structure in our organization, it might be helpful to examine whether it is a key driver behind our success or a key cause of our problems.

On the flipside, a global organization may find that it is excelling at meeting the needs of local consumers. Key drivers behind this success might be its geographic structure and its ability to manage the balance between global consistency and local customization. Or, an organization that finds it easy to quickly respond to changing customer demands may attribute that capability to a well-nurtured matrix structure.

Table 3.1 Different types of organization structures and their advantages and disadvantages

Organizational structure	Definition	Diagram/illustration	Advantages	Disadvantages
Functional structure	Functional structures are organized by function – such as marketing, sales, finance, or accounting.	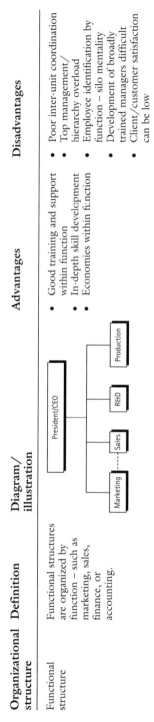	• Good training and support within function • In-depth skill development • Economies within function	• Poor inter-unit coordination • Top management/hierarchy overload • Employee identification by function – silo mentality • Development of broadly trained managers difficult • Client/customer satisfaction can be low
Product structure	Product structures facilitate cross-functional coordination by getting people within many functions focused on the product or service being offered rather than on a functional area.	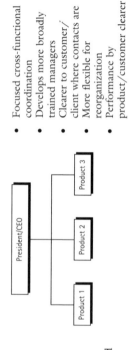	• Focused cross-functional coordination • Develops more broadly trained managers • Clearer to customer/client where contacts are • More flexible for reorganization • Performance by product/customer clearer	• Duplication/under-utilization/inefficient use of resources • Difficult to allocate shared resources • Prioritization problems • Poor exchange of info between product lines • Lose in-depth specialization/competence • Innovation tends to be restricted to product lines

Table 3.1 continued

Organizational structure	Definition	Diagram/illustration	Advantages	Disadvantages
Geographic structure	Geographic structures are organized by region.	President/CEO — North region, South region, East region	• Allows units to adapt to local circumstances • Takes advantage of local legal, political, economic differences • Training ground for general managers • Tailor products, marketing strategies to specific region	• Requires a large number of general managers • Duplication of staff services • Often difficult to maintain quality/brand equity • Innovativeness often not shared • Expatriation/repatriation costs and problems • Parent–subsidiary tensions
Matrix structure	The matrix structure attempts to combine the best of both worlds by bringing together two of the previously mentioned types of structures and attempting to overcome the downsides of each.	President/CEO — Marketing director, Sales director, Production director; Product 1 (Marketing, Sales, Production); Product 2 (Marketing, Sales, Production); Product 3 (Marketing, Sales, Production)	• Responsive • Opportunity for skill and knowledge development • Good for innovation and innovation sharing • Less likelihood of duplication (than product structure)	• Multiple bosses • Dual authority structures • Inconsistent, competing demands • Lack of accountability, everyone passing the buck • Strong interpersonal and managerial skills needed

Heads up
Look beneath the surface

Once we have a handle on how the organization chart says our organization works, we should take a step back and see if that actually maps to how our organization works in practice. How things work in practice is often called the informal structure of an organization. In determining the types of changes that need to be made to solve specific problems, the informal structure of an organization can be every bit as important as what is written down in the formal organization chart.

Coordinating across and between groups

Every type of organizational structure groups people in different ways. However, the reality is that the various groups within any organizational structure must interact in order for the organization to work. Often, organizations create structural units but fail to build processes across these structures to maximize efficiency and coordination.

For groups that are separated structurally within an organization, the use of project managers, task forces, or special ongoing teams can facilitate interaction. Regardless of the specific processes that are used to connect groups of people in our organization, these linkages are important.

In trying to determine the key drivers behind what is working well and the underlying causes of the problems, it is often beneficial to think about how much interaction is really needed between units. For example, where a lot of unpredictability or uncertainty exists, more interaction between units may be required to be able to respond quickly and effectively. From there, we can assess whether the adequate processes are in place to allow for the required amount of interaction across units.

For example, at Tween, the company is organized functionally but coordination is required across buyers, marketing, sales, and store managers. Coordination across these functional units is needed to ensure that marketing campaigns launched are geared towards customer interests, buyers are purchasing clothing that reflects customer needs, and best practices are being shared across stores. This coordination could take many forms. Brand managers might act as the point person for the marketing campaigns, ensuring that ads are contemporary, lines purchased are leading-edge, store layout is optimal, and salespeople are educated on the features of certain products. Best-practice sharing amongst stores might be covered with biannual meetings for store managers to share new ideas, and an intranet might serve to provide updated information to all the different functional groups.

People, policies, and practices

Organizational policies and practices tell us a lot about how our organization works. For starters, it would be useful to have a good understanding of the following:

- knowledge and skills of employees (education, experience, age, tenure with company, key skills)
- recruitment and selection
- training and development
- performance feedback
- career ladders (do they exist? are they vertical/horizontal?)
- rewards (profit sharing, commission, merit, individual, team, bonuses)
- benefits (health plan, vacation, work–life balance programs)
- job design (autonomy, challenge, job security).

For example, Tween might have policies of only hiring store managers with a college degree, and offering individual bonuses based on store performance to its store managers. Understanding these recruiting practices and compensation schemes along with the other dimensions of the organization, might offer possible explanations for the high turnover and the lack of information transfer among store managers.

Heads up
Reward what matters

Rewards, career ladders, and performance feedback mechanisms that are inconsistent with strategic objectives are very common causes of problems. Some companies say that innovation is key but then they don't offer incentives, time, or support for new ideas and experiments. Other organizations say that work–life balance is important but provide cell phones and laptops to all employees and ask that they be accessible at all times. Looking at how well strategic objectives align with those activities that are rewarded is often very insightful.

Physical layout

Although often overlooked, the physical layout of an organization can have a dramatic impact on the internal workings of an organization. A good place to start is to determine the locations and proximities of different groups. For example, at Tween's head office, the marketing department, the sales department, and the procurement department might all be located on separate floors of the same building. This physical layout could inhibit open communication and sharing of ideas between these various functional areas, especially when combined with a functional structure.

As part of our analysis of the internal workings of the organization, we might also want to consider the internal design of our organization and whether this design enables people to conduct business effectively and efficiently. At Tween, we might find that, in addition to functional areas being on different floors, there are limited meeting rooms available for people from various departments to come together. Or, we might discover that the HR staff are frustrated by the fact that they have cubicles but no private meeting rooms suitable for conducting activities like interviews or handling sensitive employee issues. And finally, although HR is frustrated with the rooms available to them, part of the reason advertising campaigns may be so creative at Tween is that the advertising group has funky, out-of-the-box, creative spaces for brainstorming ideas.

Culture

We can define corporate culture as the values, attitudes, norms, and beliefs that influence how an organization works. All organizations have a culture. Sometimes, a corporate culture is evident everywhere we look and actually serves as a driving force in the organization. Other times, a corporate culture is subtle and may only become apparent if we start challenging the less than obvious norms, values, attitudes, and beliefs that do exist.

Culture is a unique facet of the internal workings of our organization. On the one hand, we can consciously create culture by reinforcing certain types of values and attitudes in the everyday actions of our organization and in the ongoing stream of decisions made and by recruiting employees who align with those values. For example, some organizations might be strongly driven by a customer service orientation. Similarly, another organization might value participative decision making, input, the contribution of everyone throughout the company and giving back to the community. These choices about what the organization values may be key drivers behind what is working well.

However, culture is usually also a result of an organization's choices and decisions over time in other facets of the organization such as human resource policies, structure, and physical layout. For example, an organization that has a flat structure, an open-concept physical layout, and flexible working hours is likely to have a very different culture from an organization that is hierarchical, filled with stately, formal offices, and works strict hours. So, looking beyond values and attitudes towards other dimensions

56

of the organization may foster a deeper understanding of the dynamics of culture.

Heads up
Be conscious of the larger organizational context

As we have mentioned, it is important to analyze the culture of our business unit. However, it is also important to be conscious of the larger organizational culture in which our organization operates. Consider a proactive, charismatic store manager at Tween who has created a positive store atmosphere for customers but one that is inconsistent with the company culture. The store manager finds her approach effective within the store and believes that other Tween stores could benefit from modeling her store. However, she may face difficulties in trying to convince others that her approach is beneficial to the company if the company's overall culture dramatically differs from the culture she has created in her store. Beyond looking for differences and similarities in culture across the organization, it is also important to look beyond the organization's boundaries and to consider how regional culture or the larger societal context might influence the culture of our organization.

Technology

The world of technology is vast and rapidly changing. While it is difficult to stay on top of (never mind ahead of!) the technology in our organizations, it can have a powerful impact both positively and negatively. As we analyze our technology, there are a myriad of things we might consider. These include software applications, operating systems, hardware, database management, web development, network technologies, and telecommunications. Although it may not be necessary to bury ourselves in the technological details, it is important that we understand its role and analyze whether technology acts as a key driver to what is working well, whether technology may be a significant cause of problems, and to consider how technology might be better leveraged.

Other organizational-specific factors

Within every organization, there may be other specific factors that are also important to include in our analysis of internal workings. Therefore, as we conduct our diagnosis of the current state, we should be sure to consider those unique additional factors that may act as drivers behind what is working well, or causes of problems.

Ahead of the curve
Revisiting our initial analyses of what is working well and key problems

After we have done an initial analysis of our internal workings, we may find it useful to revisit both what is working well and the key problems in our organization to see whether they should be revised. Often, new insights about what is working well and problems emerge from the analysis of all of the different elements of the SOC wheel and their interrelationships.

PEELING BACK THE LAYERS OF THE ONION TO DETERMINE KEY DRIVERS AND ROOT CAUSES

Once we understand the internal workings of our organization and have a good idea of what is working well and what the key problems are, we can uncover the key drivers and the root causes. Getting to the core of an onion requires peeling many layers, which is just like getting to the root causes of problems and finding out the key drivers of what is working well.

Let us start with what is working well. Each time we find something that is working well, we should look to our analysis of the current state to uncover the elements that seem to be driving that success by asking, "Why does this work so well?"

If we are trying to determine the key drivers behind a particular aspect of what is working well such as high employee morale, we will know we have peeled back enough layers of the onion if we find that we have a pretty clear direction on why employees are so fired up in our company. Often, the first round of trying to determine the key drivers behind what is working well simply yields other things that are working well such as strong relations between departments, low stress levels, or satisfied employees. While uncovering this first layer gives us a little insight, it doesn't really point towards the drivers that should not be tampered with, suggesting that we need to continue peeling back the layers. When we peel back the layers further, we may find other more compelling drivers such as the fact that rewards are based on company profitability and that the organization has strong work–life balance initiatives. Another key driver behind high employee morale might be the organization's policy of not laying off any employees over the past several years, despite difficult times in the industry.

We can do a similar type of analysis for root causes. Starting with a problem, we will look to our analysis of internal workings for the causes of that problem by asking, "Why does this problem exist?" Take, for example, the problem of high turnover among store managers at Tween. By drawing on the information we have gathered about the current state of our organization, we might conclude that there are several root causes of this problem. First, the practice of only hiring store managers who have college educations might be incongruent with the salary and bonus structure currently in place. Simply put, after about a year with Tween, these college-educated managers may find they can make more money by going elsewhere. By peeling back the layers of the onion to find this root cause, we can determine that either hiring practices or the compensation plan for store managers contribute to the problem of high turnover. Second, we might realize that the structure of Tween doesn't provide a career path for the vast majority of store managers. Thus, high turnover might also stem from career ladders quickly narrowing once people move one layer up from store manager to district manager, and the fact that Tween has never considered moving store managers into corporate positions. In addition, the innovative store manager mentioned earlier may feel that it is difficult to diffuse successes given the larger culture of Tween. In short, by peeling back the layers of the onion in different dimensions of the organization, we can uncover the root causes of the problems that exist and be well positioned to determine what to harness or what to change.

Thus, two prominent reasons many change efforts fail are that the underlying causes of problems are never identified, let alone addressed, or the key drivers of what is working well are compromised or never nurtured. Most organizational problems are complex. So, whether we are digging for the key drivers behind what is working well or root causes or problems, it is useful to recognize that multiple iterations of this "peeling" process across the many dimensions (strategy; leadership; people, policies, and practices; structure/processes; physical layout; culture) is usually the best approach. Indeed, by revisiting the information gathered and continuing to peel back the layers of the onion across the SOC wheel, additional hunches about both the root causes of the problems and key drivers behind what is working well are often revealed.

Ahead of the curve
Problem-defying parts of the organization offer valuable learnings

As we work through our analysis of the current state of our organization to find the root causes, it may be helpful to learn from areas of the organization that, for some reason, are not facing these problems. These pockets of success can hold valuable insights for why problems occur in other parts of the organization, how to avoid or prevent those problems, and how to overcome them.

Key takeaways for Chapter 3

- Analyze the current state by focusing on what is working well in our organization so we don't embark on changes that could jeopardize our organization's strengths and so we can tune into changes that could further augment what is already leading to success.
- Identify key problems in our organization by considering problems at the firm level, the group level, the individual level, and problems from our customers' perspective.
- To find the key drivers behind what is working well and the root causes of the key problems we identify, we need to look at how things currently work within each of the following dimensions of our organization: strategy; leadership; structure and process; people, practices and policies; physical layout; culture, technology, and other organizational-specific factors.
- As we look for key drivers and root causes, we need to keep peeling back the layers of the onion until we find those underlying drivers that can be leveraged and those root causes that identify what needs to be changed.

Tools
Understanding the current state tool

Step 1: On the left-hand side below, brainstorm what is working well in the organization. Then determine which core capabilities and best practices are sources of sustainable competitive advantage (SCA) and which are good practices but do *not* act as sources of SCA.

**Brainstorm on what is
working well?**

**Core capabilities and best practices
that are sources of SCA**

-
-
-
-
-
-
-
-
-
-
-
-
-
-
-

-
-
-
-
-
-

**Core capabilities and best practices
that are not sources of SCA**

-
-
-
-
-
-

Step 2: Identify key problems at each level of analysis. Get input from multiple perspectives on problems by asking key stakeholders relevant to your organization or relevant to the specific change challenge you are tackling. (These might be employees, top management, customers, competitors, or others.)

Key problems

	Employees	Top management	Customers	Competitors
Individual level				
Group level				
Firm level				

Step 3: Transfer your analyses from step 1 and step 2 into the onion.shown on the following page

Step 4: Describe the current state of our organization, noting information around the wheel on the right-hand side of the figure in each facet of the SOC wheel shown on the following page.

Step 5: Return to the left-hand side of the figure, add any additional "what is working well" and "problems" to the onion.

Step 6: Now peel back the layers of the onion to uncover the key drivers of what is working well and the root causes of the problems identified. Ask the questions, "What are the key drivers underlying this strength?" or "What is the cause of this problem?" until you arrive at drivers and root causes.

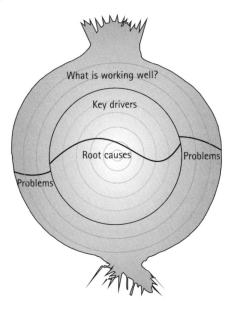

Current state SOC wheel

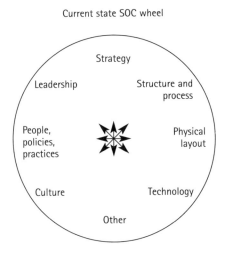

4 Building the future of our organization

This chapter draws on the diagnosis of "Where are we now?" covered in Chapters 2 and 3 and enables us to work through the question, "What changes do we need to make?" as we move into the future. We start by emphasizing external and internal factors that should be kept in mind as we build that future to ensure both short-run and long-run success. From there, a process for generating a range of possible change alternatives and evaluating these alternatives is presented. Using this process will encourage us to consider the changes in all the different facets of the SOC wheel that we need to pursue now, while simultaneously creating a powerful platform for the future. Note that in this chapter, we don't yet get into *how* changes are going to be implemented. This is covered, from various perspectives, in the remaining six chapters of the book.

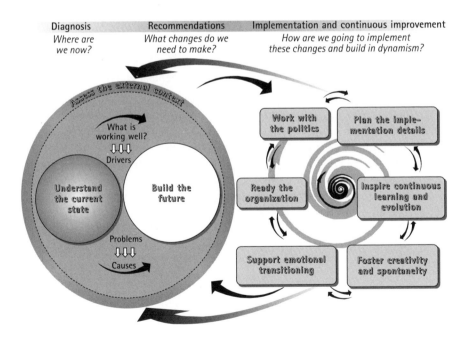

Figure 4.1 The SOC framework: building the future of our organization

At a Glance
Building the Future

- Factors that shape the future
- Creating ideas for possible futures
- Choosing the future that is best for our organization

FACTORS THAT SHAPE THE FUTURE

As we paint a picture of the future that our organization should move towards, we need to rely heavily on our external assessment to ensure that the changes we are considering position us well strategically. We also need to continually iterate back to our understanding of the internal workings of our organization to ensure that changes we are considering actually solve the key problems in the organization and build on what is working well. In addition, we will need to recognize that the future developed now will eventually need to evolve. Thus, as we try to figure out what changes to make now, we will need to keep in mind that change doesn't just start and stop. Instead, each change should be viewed as one step in our organization's evolutionary process.

Ahead of the curve
When to devote attention to building the future

A focus on building the future is especially beneficial when:

- We don't know how our organization can take advantage of opportunities in the external business environment.
- We aren't sure how our organization should respond to threats emerging from the external business environment.
- We know what things are working well in our organization and understand the key problems. However, we haven't yet determined what changes need to be made to build on what is working well and to solve the problems we have identified.
- We are in the midst of a change initiative and are feeling uncertain about whether the changes being pursued are the best course of action.

Use our assessment of the external context

To ensure that the changes we are considering position us well externally,

66

we need to draw on our assessment of the organization's external environment. This means revisiting our PEST(E) analysis and all the insights gained from our analyses of the competitive landscape, customers, and other external stakeholders from Chapter 2. This external assessment provides us with signals of what is happening outside our organization, and more importantly, gives us direction on how we can shape our future to respond to these signals. As we begin to think about that future, we will want to hone in on the specific internal changes that need to be made within each dimension of our organization to ensure success both now and in the long run.

Recall the Fresh juice company example from Chapter 2. A strategic change that was supported by an assessment of the external context was the introduction of an organic line of juices, distributed not only through grocery stores but also via specialty health food stores and cafes. This might very well be exactly the strategy that will yield Fresh long-term benefits.

However, in building the future of this company, the senior management team needs to consider the current state of the organization and the specific changes that need to be made within each dimension of the organization to support the introduction of an organic line of juices. For example, the existing organizational structure might not accommodate an additional product line, and would therefore need to be changed. Expertise in organic foods would also need to be obtained, and existing manufacturing facilities might need to be altered or expanded to accommodate the new product line.

Heads up
The beauty of being unique

As we use our analysis of the competitive landscape to consider possible directions for the future, we shouldn't feel compelled to always adopt the same approaches as our competitors. Instead, we should use this information to determine how we can differentiate ourselves from those competitors. For example, maybe all of our competitors are downsizing in response to a current recessionary period. We might be tempted to adopt the same approach. However, downsizing might dramatically undermine the long-run morale and motivation of our employees. Therefore, we might explore various options with our employees, including working reduced hours or a four-day work week for a limited period of time. It might also be the perfect time to beef up marketing efforts and steal market share from all those competitors that are caught up in the cost-cutting mindset.

Core capabilities and the future of our organization

In the last chapter, we identified the core capabilities of our organization as well as those capabilities that are sources of SCA. As we work towards building the future of our organization, we want to focus on what can make (or does make) our organization valuable, rare, inimitable, and non-substitutable by revisiting the SCACC matrix with an eye to the future.

Recall in Chapter 3 that we focused exclusively on the left-hand column of the SCACC matrix as part of our discussion of what is working well. In this chapter, we will work through all four quadrants of the SCACC matrix emphasizing implications for action.

As shown in Figure 4.2, the upper left hand quadrant is where our organization possesses the core capabilities that are sources of SCA. As we move towards the future, our suggested action in this situation is to invest time, energy, resources, and money into these core capabilities. These capabilities are strengths of the organization that we want to make sure we don't undermine as part of the changes we are planning. We also want to ensure that these capabilities continuously adapt and evolve as needed. In addition, we may want to explore whether these capabilities should be more widely diffused throughout the organization. If we return to the example of Tween, the clothing retailer introduced in Chapter 3, we might suggest that they continually invest in their ability to capture exclusive contracts with tween idols because this core capability allows them to consistently outperform other tween retail clothing chains. Tweens are drawn to their stores in a collective frenzy to buy the latest trend item endorsed and worn by their favorite tween stars.

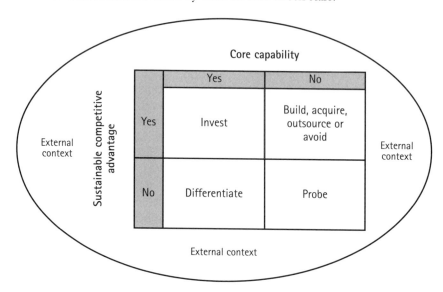

Figure 4.2 The sustainable competitive advantage core capabilities (SCACC) matrix

The upper right corner of the matrix encompasses those activities that are sources of SCA in the industry but are not present in our organization. We refer to four possible courses of action in this situation. We can attempt to build this capability slowly over time. We could also try to quickly obtain this capability through outsourcing or acquisition. Finally, we can choose to avoid the pursuit of this activity because it does not align well with our strategy.

When we see a source of SCA that is working for our competitors, our first impulse might be to scramble to possess the same capability by growing it internally, acquiring, or outsourcing it. However, attempting to grow a capability internally that our competitors have successfully leveraged on their own may pose virtually insurmountable obstacles. Similarly, while acquisition or outsourcing may seem tempting at first glance, those strategic choices often don't make sense unless they are aligned with our strategy. In addition, only organizations that are highly skilled at integration tend to succeed at these types of tactics for achieving SCA. Indeed, often in the final analysis, choosing to avoid pursuing these tactics may be the best alternative of all if they do not align well with our organization either strategically or internally.

For example, maybe one of Tween's competitors has a strong foothold in Japan, with retail outlets in all of the major cities over the past two decades. That capability originated from a long-standing relationship established through family ties years ago with one of the largest trading companies. Trying to imitate this strategy, given Tween's lack of international experience and its lack of knowledge of the Japanese market, might be extremely difficult and perhaps wasteful of critical resources.

In the bottom left corner of the matrix are those core capabilities that our organization possesses but that are not sources of SCA. These are particular activities that our organization performs quite well but no better than our competitors. Recommended actions for capabilities in this quadrant are to explore whether they can be upgraded or diversified to other areas of the organization to create sources of differentiation. Consider the following example. A large consumer food company with extensive R&D in human aging processes realized that although this core capability wasn't a source of SCA any longer in consumer foods, it offered potential for SCA in another business unit. With this in mind, it used these capabilities to develop a whole line of products for aging pets that were significantly different from any other products in the industry. They successfully reapplied something that they did well to a new arena, which resulted in big returns.

Finally, the bottom right corner of the matrix includes those organizational activities that are not done well in the organization and are not sources of competitive advantage. As part of building the future, we may want to probe and explore whether these activities could become sources of SCA in the longer run. Probing activities can include customer research, leveraging relationships with fringe stakeholders, and statistical analyses of past trends to project future opportunities. These insights would give our organization the necessary knowledge to determine whether further investment in these capabilities is recommended.

Drawing on our analysis of the current state

As we carve out the future of our organization, we will also want to work with the drivers behind what is working well and the underlying causes of problems identified in Chapter 3. Referring back to Tween, one of the key problems identified was high turnover of store managers. The current state analysis pointed towards hiring practices, advancement opportunities, compensation plans, and organizational structure as causes of this problem. To ensure that store manager turnover will decrease in the future, Tween might critically examine its recruiting practices of only hiring college graduates and consider how to create additional career ladder opportunities for store managers. Changes to compensation plans might also be considered, and maybe even changes to the structure of the organization. In short, figuring out what specific changes should be made in each of the dimensions of the current state of our organization is essential for building the future.

In addition to drawing on our problem and cause analysis, we may also want to take a hard look at the drivers behind what is working well. As noted above in the assessment of the SCACC matrix, we can often gain additional leverage by trying to nurture and further develop what is already creating high value for our organization. This means thinking about what already exists within our organization that we could build on or amplify. The additional benefit is that once we do more of what works well, often what is not working tends to recede into the background. Recall that Tween's hip and friendly customer service was a significant source of their success. The future changes Tween embarks upon should take this core capability into consideration. Any changes Tween pursues should not compromise or undermine this successful attribute. Also, part of Tween's future may entail diffusing this key success factor found in a selected number of stores to all retail outlets. Finally, Tween should explore how it might apply this formula for success to other aspects of its internal operations. For example, applying some of its learnings in customer service to relationships with its suppliers might improve the difficulties it has with obtaining trendy fashions at reasonable prices.

Ahead of the curve
Multiple causes usually mean multiple changes

Problems can range from the relatively simple to the extremely complex. For relatively simple problems, there may only be a single cause, which can be readily addressed by "tweaking" within one of the dimensions of the organization. For instance, returning to the Tween example from Chapter 3, a small change in physical layout might be all that is needed to increase the amount of information sharing between the marketing department, the sales department, and the procurement department, which are all currently located on separate floors of the same building. However, problems often have more than one cause, so we should be sure to consider changes that might need to be made within each of the facets of the SOC wheel. In the same Tween example from above, the physical layout might be only part of what is needed to solve the problem of inter-departmental communication. Other facets of the SOC wheel, such as policies (compensation), processes (better cross-functional relationships), and technology (better intranet system) might also be critical to the change.

Strive for a change-capable organization

Throughout this book, we underscore the importance of not only addressing the specific change challenge at hand but also building the longer-run capabilities needed for ongoing change. As we begin to develop possible scenarios for the future, we should try to weave in changes in the internal workings of our organization that will support continuous change, to ensure that our organizations have the change capabilities needed to succeed in the long term. For example, having a broader strategy might be beneficial to long-run success because it could enable our organization to adapt to shifts in the external business environment by modifying its strategic objectives rather than embarking on a complete overhaul of its strategy. Or maybe our organization is embedded in an extremely rapidly changing and dynamic external business environment. Creating a lean structure with simple processes that enable the organization to respond and act quickly might be one of the critical elements needed to build long-run change capabilities.

CREATING IDEAS FOR POSSIBLE FUTURES

Once we have a picture of what is happening both within the external context and the current state as well as a view of how to build long-term change capabilities within our organization, we can start to create ideas for the future. We will want to consider who should be involved, utilize some guiding principles for generating alternatives, and then create criteria for assessing those alternatives. Every change will look different, but by using this approach to build the future, we will help ensure that the changes we pursue give us a powerful platform for competitive advantage in both the short and the long run.

Who is involved in building the future?

Although there may be rare instances when we are forced to develop the future in isolation, including others in the process of building the future is recommended whenever possible. In some situations, this may involve a cascading approach where members of a task force solicit ideas from their areas and funnel them back into task force discussions. Or depending on how much time we have, working directly with a wide range of other people in generating and evaluating alternatives for the future might be possible.

For example, one useful source of ideas for building the future is the network of stakeholders with which our organization interacts. This will likely include internal stakeholders (various divisions and levels in the organization), but may also include representatives from external stakeholder groups such as customers, suppliers, distributors, government agencies, and community representatives.

Beyond stakeholder groups, we should also strive for diversity in outlook and capabilities as we build the future by ensuring that the people included in the process represent a wide range of interests and experience in the company. Diversity provides a number of perspectives and a richness of ideas that is difficult to obtain in homogenous groups of like-minded individuals.

The nature of change may also impact who should be involved. If the change we are looking at is strategic in nature and stands to impact almost all dimensions of our organization, including people from almost all areas of our organization when generating alternatives is likely to be beneficial.

Similarly, if the changes we are considering have a complicated web of drivers and causes, which point towards making changes in many dimensions of the organization, then again, we might be compelled to include a broad range of people in generating alternatives. If, however, the change we are considering appears to be quite incremental or the change involves doing more of something the organization already does well, then we might only check in casually with folks to let them know what is going on.

For example, at Tween, the problem of infighting between functional groups at headquarters appears to be a large problem with a multitude of likely causes, including training, compensation, physical layout of the organization, and structure and processes. In this case, the possible causes seem to span a wide range of dimensions of the organization, and the problem certainly impacts much of the company. Therefore, Tween would benefit from having many different people and representatives across the organization involved in generating possible change alternatives.

Ahead of the curve
Try having multiple groups generate ideas for the future simultaneously

Once we have a broad spectrum of people we would like to involve in building the future, we should strongly consider having multiple groups with diverse members simultaneously generating alternatives for the future. The beauty of this type of approach is that we develop several different visions of the future to draw upon as we work towards choosing the future that is best for our organization.

We should also consider how ideas and input are going to be gathered. Can key players in the organization meet in person to generate and discuss alternatives? Are surveys or focus groups important to gain the input and knowledge we need? Should we try a town-hall meeting, or engage in a series of informal water-cooler and coffee chats?

Heads up
Time matters

How much time we have can be a factor in determining the process for generating alternatives along with who is included in this process. If we are short on time, then we might end up doing a lot of the background work on generating alternatives and only take the time to bounce ideas off a small group of people. Or to speed things along and block out daily distractions, we could consider running a half-day offsite retreat. In contrast, if we have a lot of time, we could approach things more slowly, informally gathering ideas for change from a large sample of people in our organization.

Guiding principles for generating the "extraordinary" future

Whether we have multiple groups building the future or just a single task force, the guiding principles we use to generate alternatives can dramatically impact both the quality of the ideas obtained and people's commitment level to the change. While being able to quickly nail down a plan of action is appealing, such an approach can mean that we miss out on generating the most creative and effective ideas for our organization's future, or we lose momentum for change because folks feel they haven't been involved.

Creative ideas can come in many different forms. While we typically think of new ideas as having to be revolutionary, never-before-thought-of types of ideas, new ideas can also emerge from new ways of combining already existing processes and practices, or can stem from bringing existing ways of doing things to new areas of the organization. Regardless of the form of new ideas, generating change alternatives calls for some guiding principles that create an atmosphere of open thinking and receptivity towards ideas that are new and different. Further ideas for fostering creativity are touched on in Chapter 9 in the context of implementing strategic organizational change.

Start with a clean slate

To discover the best way to do things, it is often useful to start with a blank slate. A very radical frame of thinking can take place if the generation of alternatives begins with the premise that anything is possible. Focus on thinking about the best way to tackle problems, or amplify what is working well without any restrictions from past experience or what is already in place. In other words, encourage people to think of crazy, outlandish ideas!

Heads up
Things aren't always as they seem

We may not always know how big or small a change will be as we generate alternatives. Sometimes, problems that seem small at the outset require an elaborate process for generating alternatives because they have important implications for many facets of the organization. Other times, problems that appear overwhelming may have a narrow set of root causes that are fairly easy to resolve.

Allow for free flow of ideas

In generating alternatives, we should work hard to ensure that there is only positive, constructive criticism of ideas. We want to be open to new ideas while questioning the assumptions of old ways of doing things. It is important not to judge ideas too quickly, and instead to encourage everyone to contribute any idea they think may be possible.

Ahead of the curve
Techniques for fostering alternative generation

There are a number of techniques that can be helpful for ensuring all possible ideas are heard and considered. For instance, everyone in a meeting for generating alternatives can write down their ideas and then post them on a chart to ensure that quieter voices are heard. Giving positive feedback on all ideas as they are presented often encourages the generation of even more ideas. Alternatively, people can be divided into smaller groups and challenged to come up with the greatest number of possible ideas. Or, small groups can be assigned to drill down on the implications of alternatives about which they are already excited.

Don't be limited by self-imposed constraints

Some change leaders can miss out on new and valuable alternatives for the future because they revert back to past practices, which limit their creative abilities. People often place constraints on themselves based on assumptions they have made, which may or may not be true. So, an important guiding principle that can help uncover these types of assumptions and help open up the range of alternatives generated is to raise awareness about the negative impact of self-imposed constraints. For example, if an organization had a traumatic "restructuring" several years ago, people might hesitate to suggest further structural changes. Instead of assuming that this alternative is doomed because of past results, it is helpful to be open-minded and, at a minimum, bring this alternative to the table for evaluation. Or just because everyone else in the industry is doing something in a certain way, don't assume that is the only way or the best way. In fact, doing something different may give the organization a competitive advantage.

Don't let sunk costs scare us

When people have already invested in something – emotionally, financially, or in terms of time – there is a tendency to continue down that path because so much has already been devoted to the initiative. Raising awareness of this tendency as people generate alternatives can help ensure that certain paths or slight variations on those paths aren't the only alternatives considered. We can always include sunk costs as a part of how we evaluate the various alternatives. However, we shouldn't let sunk costs stifle good ideas at this stage of the game.

Heads up
Watch-out for talk like this!

Quotes such as the following tend to be heard in organizations that have difficulty embracing ongoing change and evolution.

- "That will never work here."
- "That's not the way we do things in this organization."

- "We don't have time for all this discussion."
- "While that sounds like a good idea, unfortunately it goes against our policy."

If we hear this kind of talk within our organization, we will likely find it challenging to engage people in the process of building the future and we will definitely have some work ahead of us when we get to the "How?" of change in shifting the mindsets to one that is more nurturing of change and evolution. If these types of attitudes are prevalent and we find them preventing the generation of viable alternatives for the future, skipping ahead to Chapter 7 to garner some specific ideas for working with the emotions of change and countering resistance may be a useful next step.

CHOOSING THE FUTURE THAT IS BEST FOR OUR ORGANIZATION

Now we have got a bunch of great ideas for possible changes that, if implemented, should support a larger strategic change, amplify what is working well, and/or effectively address the causes of problems we have identified. As we work towards choosing a future that is best for our organization, we will need to develop criteria by which alternatives can be evaluated.

What criteria should we use?

Each situation is different and the criteria we choose to evaluate each change alternative will likely be different as well. However, criteria that tend to be useful in the evaluation of many changes include:

- alignment with anticipated changes in the external context
- support of the strategic vision
- whether the change is a source of SCA
- short-run and long-run consequences
- cost
- required resources
- key stakeholder implications.

In addition, any particular change may have situation-specific criteria. For example, we may want to start with a simple look at the overall pros and cons of each alternative, giving some consideration to how easily each con can be overcome. Or, we may want to see if there is momentum around particular ideas. If many pockets of the organization have suggested a particular course of action, this convergence of ideas might suggest that the given suggestion should be highly considered. The job of a change leader is certainly much easier if everyone agrees on the changes that should be pursued. However, if we find tremendous convergence in the recommendations being generated, we might want to also explore the possibility that groupthink is occurring and that the recommendation may not actually be optimal for our organization.

Alternatively, points of divergence may arise when generating alternatives. Often this divergence sparks valuable discussions that help in the assessment of alternatives, but sometimes conflict can escalate to the point where it is counterproductive. In these situations, a useful tactic for working through these conflicting viewpoints can be to jointly develop criteria for evaluation. Consider a company that is contemplating a fundamental change in structure and is finding a great deal of divergence on how the new structure should look. One approach that a change leader might use in this situation is to try to achieve consensus on the criteria and process for evaluating the alternative structures, with an emphasis on what is best for the organization. Once agreement on criteria is created, the alternative organizational structures could be systematically evaluated along each of the criteria. This process takes out some of the emotion that can be present in a situation where there is a lot of divergence, and enables a group to move forward.

By definition

Groupthink is likely to occur when groups are highly cohesive and refers to a situation where groups desire unanimity at the expense of all else. Creative alternatives are not considered and nobody is critical of each other's ideas. The end result of groupthink is poor decision making.

Heads up
How far does our power go?

The amount of control and influence we have over a situation is also a consideration in determining which change alternatives to actually implement. If we can readily implement some change alternatives while others are completely out of our sphere of influence, then focusing on the former alternatives might be wise – at least in the short run.

Do the recommendations reinforce each other?

Once we have got support for ideas that we want to move forward with and implement, it is useful to circle back on three things. First, do the changes we are proposing reinforce other changes being considered in the organization?

Second, do our proposed changes work well with other dimensions of the existing organization? Changes often work in concert and can serve either to reinforce and support other changes or to diminish the effectiveness of other changes. For example, maybe our organization has decided to shift from a functional structure to a more geographic structure, and another high-level goal is to encourage the sharing of best practices across regions. However, a close look at a recently introduced compensation scheme reveals that rewards are based on individual and regional performance. Clearly, a shift in compensation to also include that based on company performance would be needed to facilitate the type of information sharing being sought across regions. In short, it is critical to ensure that all the recommendations and the different facets of the organization – in this case structure and compensation – work well together.

Third, have we carefully considered the implications of our proposed changes for different levels of the organization? For example, to solve the problem of high turnover of store managers at Tween, the new manager of HR might have recommended changing the compensation plan for store managers to include two more pay bands above the current maximum salary and a more generous bonus plan. However, implementing this change without looking at the compensation of people at similar levels across the organization might end up causing more problems in the long run. Rather than only high turnover of store managers, Tween might end up with high turnover of managers in general, because of the perceived inequity of these compensation plans. Taking this step and evaluating alternatives to ensure that the recommendations work together to better the organization as a whole is absolutely essential.

Ahead of the curve
Good ideas are worth keeping

Some change alternatives are worth keeping on the backburner for possible future use even though we may not want to move on the ideas now. For example, there might be an alternative that is not viable at the present time but that would be a great extension to the changes we are considering making. Similarly, another alternative that seems daunting to pursue at the moment might become more feasible as our organization moves forward and evolves.

Sometimes the "What?" and the "How?" interact

Although the focus in this chapter is on "What?" and the remaining chapters focus on "How?", a fundamental premise of this book is that change is not linear and therefore the distinction between "What?" and "How?" in real organizations is often blurred. By this point in the book, we may feel that we have developed a clear picture of the future. However, as we progress through the implementation, that picture of the future will most likely evolve. For example, once we try to implement change, maybe we won't have the resources we envisioned, or maybe people will be more resistant to change than anticipated, or perhaps by involving more people in the change, lots of new and better ideas for the future emerge. Therefore, we often need to be prepared to circle back to the "What?" even after we have moved onto the "How?" of implementing change.

Key takeaways for Chapter 4

- Use our assessment of the external context and draw on our understanding of the current state of the organization to shape the future.

- When generating alternatives for the future, develop a process that includes identifying who should be involved and promoting open thinking while trying to avoid pitfalls such as self-imposed constraints and sunk costs.

- What recommendations we pursue should be determined through a sound evaluation process that considers criteria such as anticipated changes in the external and competitive landscape, alignment with strategy and SCA, pros and cons, short-term and long-term consequences, how well the recommendations reinforce each other, cost, resource-intensiveness, implications for various stakeholder groups, and impact on the community.

- Whatever future we embark upon, we should ensure that these changes are able to adapt and evolve allowing the organization to achieve ongoing success.

- We should be open-minded and receptive to new ideas for the future that emerge even if we are already into the process of implementing change.

Tools
Building the future tool

Step 1: Using the left-hand column, think about things to keep in mind from our external and internal analyses as we build the "future."

Step 2: In the right-hand column, sketch out ideas on the processes we might use to build the future.

Things to keep in mind from our external and internal analyses	Processes for building the future
External factors	Who should be involved? (formal and informal)
	How should they be involved? (task forces, cascading approach, large-scale holistic, etc.) How will we gather ideas and input: (e.g., surveys? focus groups? in-depth interviews? observation? town-hall meetings? water cooler chats?)
Internal factors	What guiding principles should we use (start with a clean slate, allow for the free flow of ideas, watch out for sunk costs and self-imposed constraints, etc.)?
	Other ideas about what the process of building the future should look like in our organization:

Step 3: Use the left-hand column to generate alternatives for the "future." Focus on ideas that either build on "what is working well" or address the causes of the problems identified in our analysis of the current state. Also, keep in mind the assessment of the external context during this process.

Step 4: Develop criteria to use for evaluating the alternatives.

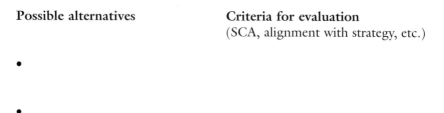

Possible alternatives

Criteria for evaluation
(SCA, alignment with strategy, etc.)

-

-

-

-

Step 5: Based on our evaluation, paint a picture of the "future." Use the diagram below to outline the changes that we recommend within each dimension of our organization.

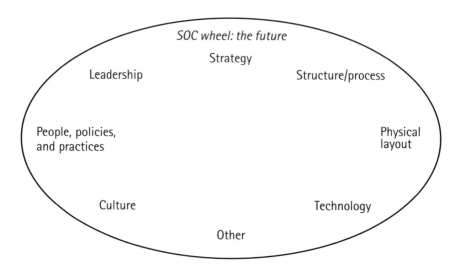

SOC wheel: the future
Strategy
Leadership
Structure/process
People, policies, and practices
Physical layout
Culture
Technology
Other

5 Getting ready for change

In the previous chapters, the focus has been on diagnosing "Where are we now?" and on developing recommendations for "What changes do we need to make?" – the first two questions of the SOC framework. In the next six chapters, the focus switches to implementation and answering the question, "How are we going to implement these changes and build in dynamism?"

By definition
Dynamism in an organizational context is defined as continuous change. Organizations that build in dynamism not only achieve success in a particular change challenge but also have the capability to learn and evolve over time.

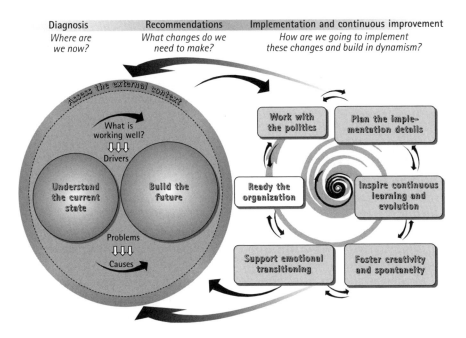

Figure 5.1 The SOC framework: readying the organization

In this chapter, we look at how readying our organization for change is a critical piece of implementation. By readying the organization, we mean ensuring we have people's commitment to change and the resources needed to make change successful.

At a Glance
Getting Ready for Change

- Are people aware of the drivers for change?
- Building the awareness needed for commitment
- Are the required resources available?
- Securing the necessary resources

Consider the following story, which some of us may have heard before. One frog is immersed in a pot of cool water, which is slowly heated up on a Bunsen burner until the water becomes hot. This frog continues to adapt to the gradual change in the water's temperature and makes no attempt to jump out of the pot, despite the fact that the water will, at some point, become so hot that the frog will die. Another frog is immersed in a second pot of water that is equally hot. This frog immediately jumps out of this hot water because it recognizes that the water is too hot to survive.

Many organizations are like the first frog in this experiment and don't realize that they are in "hot water." Maybe they aren't aware that their external business environment indicates a change is needed for the organization to survive. Or perhaps internal problems have accumulated gradually, and they don't recognize the urgency with which these problems need to be solved for the organization to continue to thrive. Obviously, we want to ensure that our organization is not like the first frog in the experiment – oblivious to warning signs in the external environment or unaware of the internal issues within the organization. We want to make sure our organizations are ready for change by raising awareness about what is driving the change and how hot the water really is. If folks understand the drivers behind the change, they are much more likely to buy in to the need for change and appreciate the urgency with which change needs to occur.

Moving away from the frog experiment, readying our organization is also about obtaining the necessary resources for a change implementation. If we don't have the money, the people, the knowledge, or the technology that is required to implement change, moving forward will be difficult, although often there are other paths to the same outcomes.

Ahead of the curve
When to devote extra attention to getting ready for change

A focus on getting ready for change is especially beneficial when:

- We have done a diagnosis, developed a picture of the future, and are ready to implement our recommended changes.
- We have ideas about how to implement a change initiative but are looking for guidance to ensure we will have the commitment and resources needed.
- We are in the midst of change and having either trouble getting folks to buy in or trouble securing the necessary resources.

ARE PEOPLE AWARE OF THE DRIVERS FOR CHANGE?

As a starting point in getting our organization ready for change, we will find it helpful to get a sense of people's awareness of the drivers for change. Here are some questions to consider:

- Are we aware of the social, technological, economic, and political trends in the external context that are driving a change?
- Do we understand how the performance and actions of competitors and other external stakeholders are pushing the organization towards change?
- Do we have access to customers' suggestions, complaints, and feedback?
- Do we have an appreciation of the problems that exist within the organization and the causes of those problems?
- Do we appreciate what is working well in the organization?

Ahead of the curve
Always be ready for change

Although the focus in this chapter is on readying our organization for a specific change challenge, ideally we want to cultivate a consistent level of readiness in our organization that enables us to mobilize the resources and commitment required to easily tackle change on an ongoing basis.

Sometimes an organization is already keenly aware of the need for change. For instance, one large ad agency might be so attuned to its largest competitor that everyone in the organization is constantly aware of every

85

competitive move. Therefore, creating the necessary readiness for change would most likely not be difficult within this organization. Or if the press has been highlighting how current practices in a manufacturing plant cause nearly toxic levels of pollution in local waterways, then folks in the plant are probably already aware and ready for change.

Ahead of the curve
Techniques for determining awareness

There are a number of techniques we can use to determine the level of awareness for change in the organization. Members of our team can listen to the grapevine or chat informally over lunch or at the water cooler. We can also collect more systematic information by administering quick on-line surveys. For example, we could ask questions such as, "How do we feel our organization is performing relative to its competitors?", or "Where do we see our market share headed in the next three years?", or more open-ended probes such as, "Do we think people in the organization would be up for a change like this? Why or why not?"

If our organization is already aware of the need for change, then we may not have a lot of work to do to convince people that change is needed. However, if our organization is not aware of the drivers for change, then we will need to build sufficient awareness before we move forward.

Heads up
Different pockets of our organization can have different levels of awareness

Looking around our organization, we will notice that there may be varying levels of awareness about what is driving a strategic change. For example, the marketing folks at a consumer foods company probably have a good sense of the latest and greatest products that competitors have been introducing to the market. Therefore, they would be ready for (and might even initiate) the introduction of a new product line. However, the production department of this same organization might not have an appreciation for this competitive driver, and so might be blindsided by the announcement of a new product line. Being sensitive to these varying levels of awareness helps ensure our entire organization is ready for change.

BUILDING THE AWARENESS NEEDED FOR COMMITMENT

If we find that our organization is not aware of the drivers for change, then we will need to spend some time building the awareness needed for commitment. To do that, we will find it helpful to draw upon our assessment of the external context discussed in Chapter 2, and our understanding of the internal workings of our organization addressed in Chapter 3.

Heads up
Don't paint too rosy a picture

We certainly want to convince people of the need for change, and one way to do this is to talk about the benefits of taking action. However, we want to be careful about painting too rosy a picture. As we build a compelling case for people to buy into, we also want to underscore that bumps and hurdles will be encountered in any change process.

Use our assessment of the external context

The assessment of the external context should highlight the macro and competitive forces that are driving the change. Taking some time to clearly outline the most compelling drivers for change and communicating them to our organization is critical for creating organizational readiness. We should also highlight the rationale that will resonate most with those involved. For instance, there might be both a social rationale and an economic rationale for implementing new environmental standards at our company. Within some pockets of the organization, the "greater good" rationale might be the most compelling, and within other pockets, the hard financial facts might be the only thing that highlights the importance of making the change. Therefore, even though both the social and the financial are driving the change, we may only choose to highlight one or the other, depending on our audience.

One vivid way to help folks get ready for change can be to project anticipated future performance based on the status quo. For example, consider a small local company that realizes it could capture increased market share by selling products online. While those inside the organization may be reluctant to make the changes, painting a picture of the success of the company undertaking this new market channel could be the catalyst needed to get them on board.

Another vivid way to help folks get on board for change is to highlight other companies that have tried similar changes and succeeded, or have some representatives from those companies come in and share their stories. For changes sparked by customer concerns, try making a videotape of real customers and their frustrations, or have some customers come in and talk about what their issues are and how they will benefit from the change.

Draw upon our understanding of the internal workings

To build commitment for a change, our understanding of the internal workings of the organization can also be useful. For example, if we analyze the internal workings of our organization and find a number of existing strengths that can further the success of the company, raising awareness will mean sharing what is working well. In some cases, this may mean sharing best practices across different areas. In other cases, this may mean doing more of what is already working well. Even if current strengths are not driving a change, focusing on what is going well can be reassuring to people within our organizations and can help build commitment, particularly if we underscore how the new change initiative will not undermine those strengths.

Drawing upon our understanding of the internal workings can also enable us to point to specific problems and their causes as other compelling drivers for change. Similar to drawing on the assessment of the external context, we want to ensure that we pinpoint the key problems that are driving change and present them in a concise and persuasive manner. For some pockets of our organization, an excellent way to ensure that people understand the drivers of change can be to show how things will run more smoothly and effectively if problems are addressed. Another powerful tool is to demonstrate what is happening with something "tangible." Maybe a shift to putting things online can be made more compelling by showing how quickly time-consuming tasks could now be done, or by stacking up the mountains of paperwork and filing that would no longer be necessary.

Ahead of the curve
The challenges of trying to be ahead of the game

Sometimes we may be initiating a strategic change that is proactive or anticipatory. Examples might include attempting to be a first mover on a breakthrough product, implementing an innovative internal management training program, creating a unique customer incentive plan, or trying to convince our organization that it would be beneficial to become more active in the local community. In these cases, building commitment may be difficult because folks inside the organization may believe that there is nothing wrong with the status quo. However, a powerful incentive in these situations may be to underscore how adopting this proactive approach would result in the company becoming a recognized leader in the industry.

Whether we are using what is working well, or problems and causes, as a catalyst for change, some useful ideas for articulating those drivers for change include:

- looking for allies and having them help with pitching the need for change
- providing lots of formal and informal opportunities for questions about why change should occur
- taking advantage of multiple communication channels (that is, company intranet, posters, bulletin boards, newsletters, lunch 'n' learns)
- ensuring that communication channels permeate all levels and groups within our organization as well as those key people that might be outside of our group but whose commitment is essential
- building in feedback mechanisms so that we can gather good input and monitor and adapt to people's reactions
- circulating visuals such as graphs and charts to highlight compelling facts and projections from the external assessment and our analysis of the internal workings
- telling a vivid story about why the change is needed, or creating powerful visuals to make the need for change come alive.

For example, maybe a group of employees are trying to convince top management that it should provide a daycare facility within the organization. Underscoring how a daycare center would make the organization a leader in the industry on work–life balance issues and address current problems through a series of open lunchtime discussions could help build commitment for change. Specific graphs and charts on how daycare would boost productivity through less stress, and the reduction of absenteeism and turnover, may provide the rationale needed for broader buy-in. Finding allies to help pitch the change as falling under values of corporate social responsibility might also help enhance readiness.

ARE THE REQUIRED RESOURCES AVAILABLE?

Another element of readying our organization for change is assessing and securing the required resources. For example, does our organization have the budget needed to implement a given change? Do we have the knowledge, skills, capabilities, and technology needed to succeed in the envisioned future?

Consider, for instance, a large copper refinery that currently uses very labor-intensive methods and wants to automate the process by which it produces copper cathodes from copper anodes. The most important resource that this organization will need to secure before worrying about anything else is the 30 million dollars worth of capital equipment necessary to automate this process.

Or, maybe additional technology and expertise needs to be secured. Take, for example, a division of a small bank facing competitive pressure to bring new, more profitable products to market. Unfortunately, the existing systems of the bank might not report on the profitability of each of the products it currently offers. If this is the case, then before this division can reasonably hope to implement changes to its product offering that will yield higher profits, training and technology may need to be secured that will report profitability on a product-by-product basis.

Ahead of the curve
Look to previous change leaders

Insights from previous change leaders can be invaluable. These people might be able to offer insight both on how to create commitment and on how to mobilize specific resources within our organization. So when determining whether the necessary resources are available, remember to ask for input from these experts.

If our organization already has the resources needed to move forward with implementing a change, then there may not be much work to do in this area. However, if this analysis shows lots of gaps between what we have and what is required to implement a given change, securing resources will be a critical component for readying the organization.

SECURING THE NECESSARY RESOURCES

If we find that our organization is lacking sufficient resources for change, we will need to devote some time and attention to securing the required resources to move forward with implementation. The tactics we take to secure each resource are going to vary, depending on the scarcity and cost of the required resource, as well as our level in the organization.

For securing particularly scarce resources, such as additional budget in a cost-conscious environment, we may have to "manage up or sideways" to convince those who oversee expenditures that the change is worthwhile and additional financial resources are necessary. In cases like these, we might try referring to the same compelling case we used to convince our organization of the need for change. Remember to consider what facts might resonate most for those people. For example, if we need to convince a senior leadership team or board of directors to allot more money to the budget in order to implement a specific change, our team might highlight how our change initiative maps onto the vision for the company or emphasize how it solves a problem that the organization has long been concerned about.

For securing other resources, we may simply need a plan and some creativity. For example, if our team is missing some key skills in our organization to move forward with a change, we might think we only have two choices – either hire additional people with those skills, or train existing people with the skills they will need to succeed in the future of our organization. However, spending time planning out what we will do to address this resource deficiency is important, and we may need to get creative, depending on our situation. For example, one creative solution might be to look at other units within our company to see if the skills our team needs exist elsewhere. If they do, perhaps there is an opportunity to do a job swap for a period of time, or bring in people from other areas of our organization to train our people.

Ahead of the curve
Don't assume we need to do it all alone

Often there can be folks within or even outside our organization who may be willing to contribute. Don't assume we need to garner all the resources needed on our own. If we make a convincing case and ask for help, unexpected assistance can often emerge. For example, maybe our organization is a not-for-profit interested in sponsoring a charity event to gain increased visibility and donations within the community. Asking for help may yield a number of resources we wouldn't anticipate. Maybe some of the key donors for our organizations hold high-level corporate positions and can provide corporate sponsorship. Maybe there are other not-for-profit organizations that would be thrilled to co-sponsor the event, and happy to kick in the resources we are having difficulty obtaining. Or maybe there is government funding available for this type of activity.

If we find that it is more difficult to secure key resources than anticipated, we may need to consider how the change initiative can reasonably proceed without those resources. Perhaps we can still move forward – only with some modifications to the plan. Maybe rolling out the change on a smaller scale is possible. This small-scale rollout could then be used as a pilot to demonstrate success and develop the support our team needs to obtain the additional resources required for a large-scale rollout.

A case in point
There may be operational solutions that don't cost money

In many cases, a lack of resources forces organizations to creatively develop solutions to particular problems. For example, consider a change that calls for launching a new product line and a lot of accompanying advertising. If advertising budget is a stumbling block, an operational solution to this challenge might be to pursue grassroots, word of mouth promotion and sampling with well-networked users, and poster board advertising versus television spots, which are expensive.

Getting ready for change is a critical aspect of change implementation, and involves both gaining commitment and securing resources. Since we don't want to be in the position of having everyone geared up for a change and then being unable to move forward, we need to make sure we consider this aspect of implementation sooner rather than later.

Key takeaways for Chapter 5

- Assess the current level of awareness of the need for strategic change using formal and/or informal methods.
- Increase people's awareness of the need for change by articulating the macro and competitive forces that are driving the change, and by highlighting the internal problems and their consequences and what is working well that should be further accentuated.
- Determine whether our team has the human, knowledge, financial, and technological resources required to move forward with implementing change.
- Be creative in developing tactics for securing the resources we need, and consider how we might modify our plan if resources are more limited.

Tools
Getting ready for change tool

Step 1: Indicate whether the organization is ready (yes) or whether attention needs to be devoted to getting ready by filling out the checkboxes below.

How ready are we now?

Are the drivers for this change clear and compelling to the people within the organization?

Drivers from the macro-environment?	☐ Yes	☐ No
Competitive drivers?	☐ Yes	☐ No
Internal drivers?	☐ Yes	☐ No

Do we have the resources required?

Financial	☐ Yes	☐ No
Human	☐ Yes	☐ No
Knowledge	☐ Yes	☐ No
Technology	☐ Yes	☐ No
Other	☐ Yes	☐ No

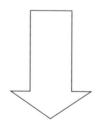

Step 2: For those drivers of change that are currently not clear or compelling, note how we can build a business case for the change in the worksheet below.

Step 3: Develop a plan for securing the resources that need to be obtained to get ready for change.

What needs to be done to be ready?

We can build a compelling business case for this change by articulating:

Macro-environment drivers:

Competitive drivers:

Internal drivers:

Worst-case scenario: Best-case scenario:
(i.e. status quo maintained)   (i.e. change implemented)

How do we secure the resources we need for this change?

Financial, human, knowledge, technology, other, etc.

6 Working with the politics of change

In every change, politics plays a role as different people jockey to represent their particular interests. Some of us love these organizational politics because of their intrigue, while some of us dislike them because of their potential to wreak havoc. However, all of us would likely agree that ignoring the politics of change is a recipe for trouble.

This chapter concentrates on another aspect of the "How?" of strategic organizational change. More specifically, we offer a systematic approach for working with the politics of change to ensure not only that the current change challenge results in success, but also that a positive platform is created for the future changes our organization will inevitably encounter.

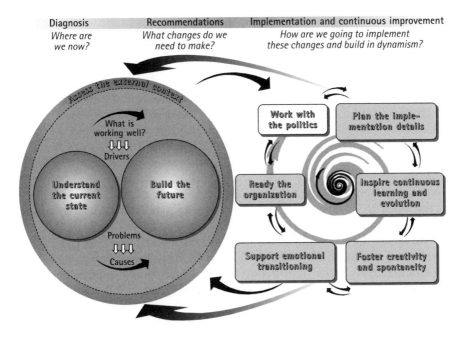

Figure 6.1 The SOC framework: working with the politics of change

At a Glance
Working With the Politics of Change

- Ignore politics at our own peril
- Which groups have an interest here?
- Who's fired up for change and who isn't?
- Tapping into key early adopters' enthusiasm
- Bringing key laggards on board
- What about those in the middle?

IGNORE POLITICS AT OUR OWN PERIL

Throughout this chapter, we will be thinking about working with the politics of change in the context of the implementation of a new customer relationship management (CRM) system at Communicorp, a large telecommunications company. Through the example of Communicorp, we see that disregarding the politics of change can prove to be disastrous while leveraging these dynamics can be highly beneficial.

A helpful starting point in working with political dynamics is to understand that everyone in organizations has distinct interests, priorities, values, and perspectives. These play out in different ways, depending on the particular change challenge being faced.

For example, consider the vice-president (VP) of marketing at Communicorp, a key member of the senior management team. He might be fired up about implementing the new CRM system because of all the additional customer information it will enable the company to collect and track.

Now imagine what happens when this VP waltzes into the call center and paints his grandiose vision of all the benefits the new CRM system will bring, without realizing that the call center employees are anxious about how this new system could impact on their jobs. Because of his lack of consideration for the call center employees' interests, a well-intentioned pitch from a high-energy, influential person in the organization falls short. In fact, the pitch ends up transforming the call center employees from a group that might have been open to change into a group of resistors who will make the change more time-consuming and difficult.

An opportunity to build momentum and enthusiasm is lost, and additional resistance to change is unwittingly created for this change, and possibly also for future changes the company may embark on. By applying the approach provided in this chapter, we see how to avoid making similar mistakes. We will understand how to effectively cultivate change – tapping into those people who are enthusiastic about a change, and working with those folks who are more reluctant.

Heads up
Make it a continual process

Gaining insight into the political dynamics of our organizations should not be a focus only during a change. Cultivating strong and trusting relationships on a continual basis creates a solid foundation that can support ongoing change and a platform from which to springboard into future change initiatives.

Ahead of the curve
When to devote extra attention to working with the politics

Although working with the politics of change is critical for all change capable organizations, it is especially beneficial when:

- we sense that people are spending a lot of time and energy speculating about the impact of a change or competing with each other at the expense of both the business and the change process
- we know of people who are excited about the change but little has been done to leverage their enthusiasm
- we believe there is a risk that negative attitudes may stifle the change process
- we want to create a receptive political climate for upcoming changes even though we are not in the midst of change.

WHICH GROUPS HAVE AN INTEREST HERE?

Within any organization there are countless groups of people, and one individual can belong to a number of these different groups. If we think about our organizations, most employees probably belong to a functional area or product group, and also align with a particular level within the organization. For instance, the VP of marketing at Communicorp likely considers himself to be part of the marketing group and also part of the top management team of the company. In addition, he may be a member of some informal groups, such as the company softball team or social committee.

By definition
Interest group: a cluster of people impacted in a similar way by a given change. Although the interest groups that emerge may vary with each change, some common ways that people align during change include:

99

- by level within the organization (i.e., top management, middle management, frontline employees)
- by functional area (i.e., marketing, finance, IT)
- by length of service or history with the company (i.e., old-timers, new hires)
- by organizational units (i.e., head office, business units, divisions)
- by membership (i.e., unions, salespeople of the year, company sports team)
- by personal beliefs and values (i.e., about their work, what is best for the organization, and the larger community).

Although people usually belong to a number of different groups within their organization, the groups that people align with for a particular change is what matters when we are working with the politics of change. The key interest groups that emerge will vary, depending upon the benefits, gains, and losses that are perceived. For instance, the call center manager at Communicorp might align with her call center team when confronted with the implementation of the new CRM system. However, she might align with the management team for a change to compensation packages.

How do we know an interest group when we see one?

Interest groups come in all shapes and sizes. A good way to identify the relevant interest groups for a specific change is to consider:

- Which groups perceive that they will benefit from this change?
- Which groups perceive that they will be negatively impacted by this change?

At Communicorp, some groups that would be likely to perceive benefits from implementing a new CRM system are the marketing department and senior management team. Marketing folks are probably thrilled about all the new pricing plans and promotions that can be developed with the additional customer information the new CRM will provide to them. Similarly, senior management is probably excited about the strategic insights this new customer information may reveal.

On the flip side, a group that likely perceives negative impacts from the new CRM system is the call center employees. These people are probably anxious about having to learn a new system, and may also be worried that handling each customer call will take longer, given the increased amount of customer information that the new system requires them to enter. They may also be concerned that the tracking and monitoring required by the CRM system will leave them less time to spend developing a personal rapport with their customers.

> ## Heads up
> *Go beyond the obvious*
>
> Some potentially important interest groups such as customers, suppliers, lobbyists, and the outside community are easy to overlook because they don't appear on our organizational charts. Since groups such as these may be important to the success of a given change, we need to remember to use a broad perspective when searching for interest groups that are relevant. Often, key outside stakeholders from previous change initiatives are also relevant for subsequent change initiatives. In addition, they may have useful learnings, advice, and tips on how to work with the political dynamics.

How do we know what various groups' interests are?

Once we have identified groups of people who perceive potential benefits or potential drawbacks to a change, it is likely that we will have a sense of their interests. However, we shouldn't assume we can fully understand various groups' interests from only our vantage point. We should talk with these various groups to learn more about what they perceive to be the specific advantages or disadvantages of the change.

We can do this informally at the water cooler or in a more formal manner. With the latter approach, we might have meetings or conduct focus group sessions to discuss the change. Sometimes, it can also be useful to have an impartial outsider come in to facilitate these types of sessions to ensure candid discussion. The objective, no matter what approach we use, is to gain a true understanding of each group's interests and also an understanding of *why* they feel the way they do. Only then can we begin to create a change process that reaches them, resonates with them, and cultivates the ongoing commitment needed for long-term success.

Which interest groups are most relevant?

Since we may have identified a large number of interest groups, narrowing in on those groups most essential to the success of a given change helps us to determine where our time and energy is best spent. To prioritize those interest groups we might consider:

- Which groups' cooperation, expertise, resources, or influence is most important for the success of the change?

101

- Which groups' opposition could be particularly detrimental to the success of the change?

Returning to Communicorp, the call center employees are a group whose cooperation and expertise can make or break the success of the change. Their cooperation is essential for the smooth implementation of the new CRM system, and since they are intimately familiar with the shortcomings of the current system, their input is essential for customizing the new system. However, as we have established, they are likely to be reticent about this change. Since their anticipated opposition to the new CRM system could completely derail this change, the call center group is perhaps one of the most "interesting" of the interest groups in this example. Time spent working with this group is definitely worthwhile and essential for cultivating long-term change capabilities.

The marketing department is another group that is important to the success of this change. It can provide valuable input on the design of the new CRM system because the staff know what customer data, if collected, can benefit the business. Since they are likely to be positively predisposed to the change, this group likely requires less time and attention than the call center group. However, keeping this group on board is still essential.

Heads up
Key interest groups aren't static

Interest groups have a way of evolving throughout any change process. A group that might be important in the early days of a change might eventually fade into the background. Conversely, a group such as IT might emerge as important later on, as the technological implications of the change become more apparent.

WHO'S FIRED UP FOR CHANGE AND WHO ISN'T?

With any change there are key interest groups that tend to have different views on the upsides and the downsides of a particular change. Understanding these groups and their interests is important, since this gives us hints about where key pockets of resistance and enthusiasm are likely to reside.

However, to effectively work with the politics of change, we need to move beyond the group level and hone in on the individuals we need to work with for a particular change. This involves identifying both the people within key interest groups who are influential and particularly enthusiastic about the change, and also those more reticent about change.

Early adopters

The people within key interest groups who are fired up about the change can be thought of as early adopters. They are quick to adapt to change and can be helpful in mobilizing other folks inside the organization towards change. The first place to look for early adopters is within those key interest groups that perceive that they will benefit from the change.

For example, the marketing department of Communicorp probably views the change positively since its staff perceive that, as a group, they will benefit from a new CRM system. Looking within that group, the VP of marketing might stand out as an important early adopter since he happens to be the main champion for implementing the new system. He is excited, enthusiastic, and has already managed to convince the rest of the senior management team of all the benefits a new CRM will bring. Given his enthusiasm, the influence he has in the company, and his network of relationships, he could be essential for fueling additional enthusiasm for this change.

> ## By definition
> Sociologist Everett Rogers identified several distinct groups that emerge in any process of innovation in his book entitled *Diffusion of Innovation* (New York: Free Press, 1962).
> *Early adopters*: The approximately one-sixth of people who welcome change and are easily convinced of its merits.
> *Middle majority*: The approximately two-thirds of people who look to their peers before taking a stance.
> *Laggards*: The approximately one-sixth of people who are more reluctant or resistant to change.

Laggards

The folks within key interest groups who are resistant to the change can be thought of as laggards. However, it's important to distinguish between folks who lag behind in support of a change for good reasons and folks who are laggards regardless of what change they are facing. People who are laggards for good reasons resist change because they genuinely believe there are flaws in what is being proposed or how it is being implemented. These laggards are critical to listen to. They can be a catalyst for useful rethinking of the change. They may offer an alternative approach, provide the devil's advocate viewpoint, or prompt the questioning of fundamental aspects of the change.

Returning to Communicorp, the call center is a key interest group that would likely be more negative about the change. Within that particular group, there may be a team leader who is highly skeptical of the need for any new system in her department because she feels her employees are very responsive to customers and that "some new technology" is only likely to hamper service representatives' ability to cultivate positive customer relationships. If this individual also happens to be the pitcher of the company softball team, then she will have many well-established ties with a variety of people throughout the organization and her negative views might create major backlash for the change initiative.

Taking the time to work with her team and solicit ideas about how the information provided by the CRM system might be used to build better customer relationships could be very helpful. We might also want to gather input from the team leader and her team on how to approach the implementation of the CRM system, or even consider making her a key point person. These actions would confirm the organization's interest in the team leader's perspective, and help build her and her followers' commitment to the change.

On the other hand, sometimes laggards emerge that tend to resist change regardless of the purpose, value, and approach of the change. Often these people have underlying fears or anxieties about change that we need to help them work through. The next chapter addresses these emotional issues in more depth.

By definition

Network concepts taken from the field of sociology have recently been applied to business, and can be useful for identifying key influencers in organizational change.

Central connectors: These are "informal" go-to people who have associations and influence with a large number of people in the organization.

Information brokers: These people are well plugged into other networks because of their ability to provide accessible information.

Boundary spanners: Those who have far-reaching links across various groups.

Although we often find key networkers within the relevant interest groups, sometimes there are central connectors, information brokers, and boundary spanners who are helpful for the change in interest groups that are more peripheral to the change.

Outliers

While many people align with the disposition of their interest groups, we also want to be on the lookout for exceptions to this rule. For example, influential early adopters can sometimes be found even in those interest groups that perceive negative impacts from the change. There might be a really popular call center service representative that has a passion for all things technological. For this person, the new CRM system is exciting and represents a great opportunity to get some hands-on experience with cutting-edge technology. So although the call center group as a whole may tend to be resistant to the new CRM system, if we identify this early adopter – who also happens to play the important role of being a central connector in the call center – we may find a great supporter who can help facilitate the change process.

Similarly, laggards can sometimes be found even in those interest groups that perceive benefits from the change. An outlier within the senior management team at Communicorp might be the VP of finance. A long history of heated debates about the bottom-line results likely to be generated from new marketing initiatives may have left her reluctant to jump on board with the VP of marketing's latest pet project. What makes the VP of finance a particularly important outlier to get on board sooner rather than later is the fact that her opinions are always well regarded by the CEO.

Ahead of the curve
Look to previous change receptivity for insight

It's useful to recognize that there may be consistent patterns in how people tend to react across different change initiatives. For example, there may be a group of people that tend to be open to change unless there are good reasons not to be supportive of change. And conversely, there may be patterns in who tends to react negatively to change. Often it is helpful to remember these groupings when we are developing strategies for how to leverage support for change or work with resistors.

TAPPING INTO KEY EARLY ADOPTERS' ENTHUSIASM

Tapping into the enthusiasm of early adopters – especially those with a lot of influence – can be extremely helpful in moving change forward. Since early adopters are quick to get on board with a change, they can help build commitment, buy-in, and momentum throughout the organization. They can also help reduce the resistance to change that might exist and assist with solving problems that arise throughout the change process. Another benefit of tapping into these folks' enthusiasm is that great ideas pertaining to the change will emerge.

Key early adopters can be the seeds that enable enthusiasm for change to grow throughout our organizations – not only for this particular change but also for the ongoing stream of changes our organizations will inevitably encounter. Because these key people tend to be well connected, they can have an exponential impact on fueling enthusiasm and tempering resistance. Although tapping early adopters might appear to be time-consuming, their ability to seed and spark change can lead to it progressing more quickly in the long run.

So how can we tap into key early adopters? There is a range of options we can pursue. What options to pursue will depend on the type of change being faced and how far along we are in the change process. As a start, consider some of the following.

Ask them for input

People who are excited about a change are often great sources of input. They are likely to have ideas about both what to do and how to do it – and are usually more than happy to share those ideas with anyone who might listen! Whether we seek input in one-on-one conversations or as part of a more structured focus group, giving early adopters the opportunity to provide input yields excellent ideas. Equally important, the process of seeking input cultivates commitment to the change and generates positive buzz, which can ripple through the organization and help build momentum.

Test out ideas on them

If we are pressed for time or want some quick feedback on certain elements of the change process, testing out ideas with some key early adopters is a great way to not only fuel the momentum for the change process, but also gain some valuable insights. Moreover, the process of including them in this way will likely solidify their commitment to the change.

Enlist them to better package or sell the change

Another really useful way to draw on key early adopters' enthusiasm is to ask for their advice on how to best package or sell the proposed change. Since these folks are enthusiastic and well connected, it is tremendously beneficial to obtain their unique insights about various aspects of the change process. For example, key early adopters might have useful opinions on the communication strategies most likely to succeed, the types of benefits that may resonate most, and the best ways to go about alleviating anxiety about the change.

Empower them to lead parts of change

Some key early adopters may have skills or knowledge that could be helpful in specific aspects of a given change. What better way to tap into the enthusiasm of these folks than to leverage their skills and knowledge and give them room to actually lead these aspects of the change? This is a sure way to have early adopters spread their enthusiasm to other people in the organization. Moreover, when folks are empowered to lead certain aspects of change initiatives, long-run change capabilities tend to be cultivated. People in the organization develop skills in leading change, and they are fired up for ongoing change because they have been given the opportunity to help mold change and contribute to the organization's success.

Ahead of the curve
Try a TMT

Consider creating a transition management team (TMT) to act as the steering committee for the change. TMTs generally include representatives from a diverse range of interest groups, and are used to ensure that varied interests are recognized and incorporated into the change process. You might also think about creating an ongoing task force within your organization, whose mandate is to support the organization's various change initiatives. This will allow learnings from one change to be passed on to the next change.

Ask them to provide coaching and education

Another way to tap into the enthusiasm of key early adopters is to recruit them to play a coaching or mentoring role throughout the change process. In this kind of role, the early adopter can offer direct hands-on advice as well as influence the attitudes of those they interact with because of their new role.

BRINGING KEY LAGGARDS ON BOARD

Key laggards can have a dramatic impact on how a change progresses. If their interests are never given consideration and efforts are not made to bring them on board, they can create negative momentum that can slow things down, undermine success, and turn minor hurdles into major roadblocks. It is wise to start working with key laggards sooner rather than later, to address their issues and concerns. Even though this step might take time in the short run, in the long run this change and subsequent changes will evolve more quickly and smoothly.

So how can we bring key laggards on board? There are many potential approaches, depending on the situation. Here are some to try.

Step into their shoes

Laggards can really dig their heels in if they feel their views about a particular change are being ignored. While most of us wouldn't intentionally disregard the interests or opinions of anyone, it is important to consciously step into the shoes of key laggards so that we can understand their point of view and work with them more effectively.

Recall how the VP of marketing at Communicorp botched his initial communication with the call center about the new CRM system. If he had taken into consideration the perspectives of those people in the call center, his communication could have yielded better end results. He then might have actively addressed concerns about increased workload and how customer relationships would be enhanced with the new CRM system. He might also have tempered his raw enthusiasm for the project to leave room for dialogue about the proposed change. So by stepping into the shoes of key laggards in the call center, the VP could have made inroads to bringing the whole call center on board rather than creating unnecessary resistance.

Focus on interests instead of positions

Often, people get locked into being either "for" or "against" a change. A useful tactic for helping laggards move away from the position of being "against" a change is to uncover why these people have chosen that position. Once we discover why they oppose the change, it becomes easier to brainstorm options or find paths that help move them towards the change. It is also important to explore underlying interests, because buried in the anxiety and concern of key laggards can be valuable insights that end up being essential to the success of the change.

For example, imagine someone who is "against" a change in an organization. Perhaps the underlying reason for this position is a fear that the person lacks the skills needed to do the job well in the changed environment. If we understand this underlying interest, possible solutions might emerge such as additional training or weekly feedback sessions, which would enable this key laggard to overcome the fear of change and get on board, while improving the change process for the entire organization.

Cast the change in a new light

Often laggards resist change because they can only see its immediate impact on them. Painting a picture of how a particular change connects to larger goals of the company can sometimes be persuasive in getting key laggards to see a change in a more positive light.

For example, we might try reframing a change to highlight how it contributes to the long-run viability of the company. Specifically we could show how the change helps the company beat the competition, achieve market share goals, and enhance customer service. Returning to the Communicorp example, for those folks who believe that the CRM system will leave less time for developing a rapport with their customers it might be important to shine a light on how this new CRM system will help the organization better meet their customers' needs.

Ahead of the curve
Appeal to people's hearts

Demonstrating how a change aligns with larger societal goals and subsequent personal values can also help some laggards shift their views.

For instance, perhaps line workers at a manufacturing plant perceive changes in the manufacturing process to be negative. Highlighting how the changes have positive environmental impacts and serve to improve air quality in the surrounding areas might resonate for some laggards, and help them to see the change in a more positive light.

Learn and practice the art of active listening

Whenever we are speaking with someone, it is easy to focus on what we want to say next rather than on what the other person is saying. When we are speaking with laggards, it can be particularly tempting to fall into this trap as our mind races to come up with persuasive arguments in support of the change.

Active listening is a useful technique for conveying to another person that we have heard and understood their situation. Basically, our goal is to echo back to the person what we think we have heard and to seek confirmation on our understanding.

Ahead of the curve
Phrases for active listening

If we want to confirm our understanding through active listening, we might use phrases such as:

- "What I hear you saying is ..."
- "If I understand correctly, you ..."
- "So let me play back to you what I think I've heard ..."

Find something to agree upon

We might think that with some key laggards, we will never find anything that can persuade them to get on board with a change. A useful approach with these folks is to try to find something (anything!) to agree upon. For example, while we may not be able to get them to agree on the fundamental direction of the change, they just might agree to some small aspect of the change process such as holding a town-hall meeting to share ideas. The hope is that once they agree to one small thing, it will be easier to get them to agree to bigger things and begin to contribute to the change.

And if all else fails...

The reality of strategic organizational change is that we may find ourselves

By definition

Tipping point: Malcolm Gladwell's book entitled *The Tipping Point: How Little Things Can Make a Big Difference* (2000) highlights how a handful of influential people can start and sustain big shifts in human behavior. The idea of the tipping point is useful for understanding how to fuel change. The point at which a handful of people (early adopters) create enough momentum that it starts to spread like wildfire can be thought of as the tipping point in change. The key for change leaders is to ensure that the middle majority tipping point is aligned positively with change.

having to accept that some folks will never be "on board" with a particular change. If we have tried many of the approaches described above and have not had any luck, we might feel like throwing our hands up in the air and walking away from them. While ideally our hope would be to get everyone on board, what might make sense with these more difficult laggards is to think about how to minimize their negative impact.

Returning to Communicorp, maybe we know that one of the key laggards is fixated on the inadequacy of current workstations if the new CRM system is implemented. Although circulating information on how workstations will be adapted to accommodate the new system may not overcome this particular laggard's anxiety, it might be a useful preemptive tactic with others that could prevent this key laggard from being able to make workstation layout a huge issue with others.

WHAT ABOUT THOSE IN THE MIDDLE?

In between the early adopters and the laggards is the biggest group of all: the middle majority. The good news is that this middle majority tends to look to others for what they should do. By focusing in on fueling the early adopters and working with the laggards, we can usually find the "tipping point" that swings the middle majority towards getting on board.

Key takeaways for Chapter 6

- Political dynamics emerge throughout every change initiative. This change and subsequent changes will be more successful if we work with these politics rather than ignore them.
- A first step in working with the politics of change is to identify the key interest groups that are involved in a particular change, and understand their interests.
- A next step in working with the politics of change is to find the folks within each of the key interest groups that are most influential: the key early adopters and the key laggards.
- By tapping into the enthusiasm of key early adopters we can leverage their positive energy and build momentum for change.
- By working with laggards and understanding their reasons for resistance, we can uncover beneficial improvements to the change, win their support, and cultivate the commitment needed for long-run success.
- By working with both groups, we can usually swing the tipping point of the middle majority to create positive alignment towards change throughout our organizations.

Tools
Working with the politics of change tool

Identifying interest groups, early adopters, and laggards

Step 1: Order the key interest groups involved in this change and note their interests.

Step 2: Identify key early adopters and laggards within each interest group.

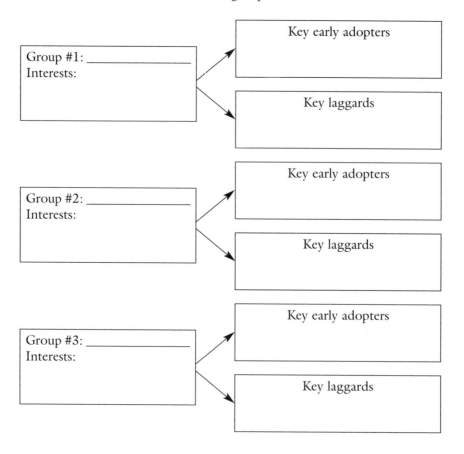

Group #1: _____
Interests:

Key early adopters

Key laggards

Group #2: _____
Interests:

Key early adopters

Key laggards

Group #3: _____
Interests:

Key early adopters

Key laggards

Mobilizing key early adopters

Step 3: Copy key *early adopters* from each interest group into the appropriate lines below.

Step 4: Generate ideas for effectively tapping into these individuals' enthusiasm to fuel change.

Interest group #1: _____

_____ →

_____ →

_____ →

Interest group #2: _____

_____ →

_____ →

_____ →

Interest group #3: _____

_____ →

_____ →

_____ →

Working with laggards

Step 5: Copy the key *laggards* from each interest group into the appropriate lines below.

Step 6: Generate ideas for helping these individuals get "on board."

Interest group #1: _____

_____ ⟶ ☐

_____ ⟶ ☐

_____ ⟶ ☐

Interest group #2: _____

_____ ⟶ ☐

_____ ⟶ ☐

_____ ⟶ ☐

Interest group #3: _____

_____ ⟶ ☐

_____ ⟶ ☐

_____ ⟶ ☐

7   Supporting emotional transitioning

Everyone reacts differently to a particular change. Some people may embrace change and be excited, hopeful, and enthusiastic. Others may fear change, be confused, angry, or not quite know what to feel. As change leaders, we need to recognize that everyone takes their own personal journey through the emotions of change and that they take this journey at their own pace. Spending time on the emotional aspects of change and helping people transition is critical for successfully cultivating change in our organizations. Although there is no easy recipe, this chapter offers many approaches for helping people make the transition through the emotions of change more easily and more successfully. By helping people work through their emotions, we create a better platform for current changes and improve receptivity to future changes.

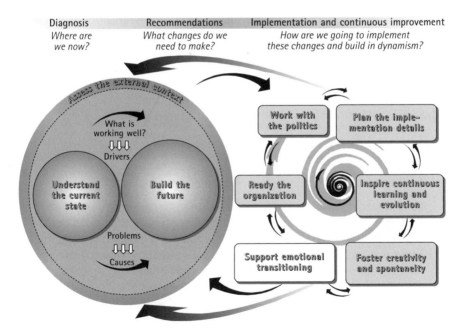

Figure 7.1 The SOC framework: supporting emotional transitioning

At a Glance
Supporting Emotional Transitioning

- The emotional journey of change
- People start at many different places on their journey
- Figuring out where people need to be for change to succeed
- Understanding the "Why?" underneath emotions
- Exploring action steps to support transitioning

THE EMOTIONAL JOURNEY OF CHANGE

Throughout this chapter, we will picture ourselves in the role of VP of the small business lending division at One-Bank. Top management has recently announced that our bank is merging with another large bank to form a new entity called Two-Banks. Some folks in our organization are thrilled with this merger because they believe it will open up new career opportunities, wake up the organization, and enable it to better compete in the industry. Others are petrified because they are worried that they will lose their jobs, or that they will have to work with new people and lose the good working relationships they currently enjoy. Many may be feeling overwhelmed or simply confused about what exactly the merger will entail in the months to come, and some are just plain angry that life in the future won't look like it does today. With every change comes emotion, and a merger of two banks is certainly no exception. At its core, change is about people making a transition from where they are now to something new or different. For some people, this transition from the old to the new is relatively easy, while for others, letting go of the way things are currently done to move towards the unknown and reinvest in a new reality is a scary proposition.

Heads up
Beware of some common myths about emotions

Some change leaders view emotions as "noise," or see emotions as being irrational and so choose to ignore them. In contrast, enlightened change leaders assume that emotions are important and should be validated. These people recognize that attempting to sweep emotions under the rug will only backfire. They also know that emotional reactions are grounded in rational thinking, and that it is essential to support those that are fearful, concerned, or worried about change in order for people to be willing to reinvest in a new reality and for change to effectively move forward.

Ahead of the curve
When to devote extra attention to supporting emotional transitions

Although supporting emotional transitions is critical for all change capable organizations, it is especially beneficial when:

- we feel like we haven't got a good understanding of how folks in our organization are reacting to change
- we sense a wide range of emotions emanating from the change but don't know how to deal with all of them
- we sense that many people in our organization are experiencing negative emotions such as fear, worry, stress, anger, and anxiety about moving from the current state to the future
- we personally are experiencing negative emotions about a change and wish to better understand those emotions and how we might work through them.

PEOPLE START AT MANY DIFFERENT PLACES ON THEIR JOURNEY

People's immediate reactions upon finding out about an impending change can vary quite dramatically. Usually a combination of factors such as their role in the change, the likely consequences of the change, the sentiments of their peers towards change, and other personal factors will play a role. For example, a VP at One-Bank might have heard the following range of comments around the water cooler during the afternoon that the merger was announced:

- "This company needs a shake-up and I, for one, can't wait to see how things unfold!"
- "I don't know what to think."
- "I've been through a merger before and, trust me, this is going to be nothing but bad news."

The first reaction noted above appears to be from a person who sees the change as a necessity and is eager for the merger to occur. This individual seems to easily see the benefits of the merger, and overall emanates a "You betcha!" type of attitude towards the change.

The second reaction comes from someone who is obviously reticent about expressing positive emotions about the change. This person might agree in principle, seeing benefits to the merger, but may be hesitant about having to give up personal comfort zones and not be ready to take the leap into action. He or she might be hesitant about the change because he or

117

she needs more information, or is concerned about how the change will impact him or her directly. A phrase that seems to fit the emotion here is "Do we have to?"

The third initial reaction to the merger expresses an overall "Not a chance" type of attitude. This individual appears to be reluctant to engage or take action. This reluctance may stem from emotions such as denial, shock, fear, anger, and confusion. Understanding the reasons why this person feels the way he or she does, and supporting this person and others who feel similarly, will be particularly critical for the change to be successful.

Ahead of the curve
Political interests often align with emotions and vice versa

In the last chapter, the politics of change were explored. Not surprisingly, emotional reactions to change often align pretty closely with political reactions. So, those folks that have a "You betcha" attitude towards a change tend to be the early adopters in a change, whereas those folks who have a "Not a chance" attitude tend to be the laggards. And finally, those with a "Do we have to?" attitude tend to be swayed by the most influential interest groups.

While we don't discount the complexity and range of emotions, to gain insight into the emotions that people within our organization may be experiencing, it can be helpful to try to identify where specific individuals are emotionally across these three categories. Are they at "You betcha!," "Do we have to?" or "Not a chance"? Without some sort of classification, the web of emotions that arise from organizational members may limit our ability to move the change forward. From there, we may want to figure out where they need to be for the change to be successful. Then we will want to work with them to understand why they feel the way they do, and determine how the organization might be able to best support them during the change. We may also want to note other key factors that may be impacting them emotionally. For example, maybe the reason someone is having difficulties coping with a new change is because he or she has recently gone through a divorce and therefore finds it difficult to cope with any other changes in their life at that time.

Heads up
Don't assume

Making assumptions about how people are feeling about a change can lead to misunderstandings. Check with people directly to see how they are feeling. Exploring why they feel the way they do about the change will help us develop possible action steps that may help them cope with, or even become enthusiastic about, the change.

This process will allow us to understand the dynamics of emotions within our organization, and enable us to discern the best approaches for helping people within our organization make the transition towards change. Note that throughout the process of working with emotions, our focus should be on individuals, to understand why they feel the way they do and to help them become more at ease with moving forward with the change.

Ahead of the curve
The change process impacts emotional transitioning

While this chapter focuses exclusively on the emotions of change, actions stemming from the other chapters in this book may also positively impact folks' emotional reactions to change. By taking steps such as including folks in the process, maintaining open communication, underscoring the drivers of change, and reducing political conflict, we create a positive climate for change, which can serve to lessen the negative emotions people feel towards a particular change challenge.

Ahead of the curve
We can't do it all

We may not be able to help everyone in our organization transition through the emotions of change. We might not have enough time, some people might not open up to us, or we might find it difficult to relate to someone interpersonally. What we can try if we are short on time is to work with our direct reports to help them make the transition through the emotions they are experiencing about the change, then train them to work with their direct reports, and so on.

If we are not sure that we have the skill to help people make the transition emotionally, we might try simply acting as a sounding board, or we might try finding someone else on our team who can help people process the emotions associated with a change. These types of approaches ensure that everyone in our organization receives some support in moving through their emotional journey.

For those folks that are at the "You betcha!" stage of their emotional journey through change, our role as change leader is to keep them positive and enthusiastic. Since we are not going to need to spend a lot of time helping them make the transition through the emotions of change, look at Chapter 6 for ideas on how to best leverage their optimistic attitudes towards the change. However, we will need to support those folks that express "Not a chance" or "Do we have to?" types of emotion, as they work through their reactions. This emotional support will make an important contribution to the success of a given change challenge, and will also make future changes progress more smoothly.

FIGURING OUT WHERE PEOPLE NEED TO BE FOR CHANGE TO SUCCEED

While we might like everyone in our organization to be at "You betcha!", the reality is that not everyone needs to be extremely positive and enthusiastic about a change in order for the change to be successful. In fact, it might be enough for certain people to simply be aware of the changes, and be sufficiently positive that they won't interfere. Knowing where different people in our organization need to be on their emotional journey for a change to be successful can often be a very useful step in supporting folks in their transitioning. Once we have a pretty good sense of where they need to be for change to move forward, we will want to strive to provide the support they need to help them get there.

UNDERSTANDING THE "WHY?" UNDERNEATH EMOTIONS

To support the transition of those "Not a chance" and "Do we have to?" folks in our organization towards change, we will need to start by acknowledging that feeling a range of emotions throughout the change process is normal. A wide variety of emotions are to be expected, and we will need to convey to people that it is okay to be experiencing the emotions they are feeling. This step serves to open up the lines of communication with the people in our organization. They may be more likely to openly express their feelings because we have validated that the emotional dimension of change exists and is significant.

Heads up
Beware of email

Email communication, while efficient, can easily be misinterpreted and does not allow for monitoring reactions or for two-way exchange. Therefore, we might find that good old-fashioned face-to-face interaction is the best route when we are trying to support people in our organization so that they can make the transition through the emotions of change.

Being patient, accessible, and approachable to the people in our organization throughout a change process is also very important, and can encourage the free and open dialogue that will enable them to more easily make the transition towards a new future. As change leaders, we need to ensure that our actions send the right message. For instance, we might try spending time walking around and talking with the people in our organization about the change, and when we do need to be in our office, consider leaving the door open. An open door sends a strong message that we are available to help people process what the change means for them. This type of openness not only enables us to help people transition through the emotions of change, but will also help us uncover insights and action steps that can dramatically improve a change process.

However, to really work with the emotional dimension of change, we have to delve deeper than acknowledging people's emotions and opening the lines of communication. To be able to provide the support needed to help folks in our organization feel more positively about a change, we will need to uncover why people feel the way they do. Typical reasons that people experience negative emotions about a change include not understanding the change or the drivers for the change; fearing job loss, loss of status, or lack of skills; doubts about the abilities and motives of the change agents; lingering negative effects from previous poor change experiences; and questions about whether the proposed change is sound. Each of these is discussed below. Additional detail on both fear factors and possible actions steps are provided and summarized in Table 7.1.

EXPLORING ACTION STEPS TO SUPPORT TRANSITIONING

In this section, each of these typical concerns is discussed in more depth and possible action steps to address each concern are highlighted. By understanding the reasons behind people's emotions, we will be better equipped to support them in making the transition to where they need to be for change to be successful.

Overcoming lack of understanding for the need for change

One of the most common reasons people experience negative emotions about a change is that they don't understand the need for change, or haven't been convinced that the change is a good idea for their company.

For example, a VP at One-Bank might hear people in the small business lending division say things like, "I'm really confused, I don't understand why this merger is a good thing for One-Bank", or "I'm personally content with what we're doing in the company right now." Comments like these

Table 7.1 Fear factors and possible action steps

Understand "Why?"	Possible action steps
"I don't understand this change." • why it is happening • what it is • how it will transpire.	Communicate the external and internal drivers for change. Involve folks in the "What?" and the "How?"
"I'm worried I don't have the skills required."	Provide training. Establish ongoing feedback loops.
"I'm not sure the people running this change know what they're doing."	Build credibility with past successes, add "power" to the team, involve skeptics Reassess whether criticisms hold merit.
"This change is too risky and too costly."	Demonstrate the long-run benefits associated with the change. Explore whether there are ways to minimize risk and reduce cost.
"Change never works in this place, what makes this one any different?"	Disassociate this change with previous changes by emphasizing differences in the nature of change, who's leading the change, the process of change, etc.
"I've worked hard to get where I am, and this change is going to mess this all up."	Dig deeper on what they think is going to be messed up. Underscore the positive of "what is in it for them." If there is uncertainty, be open and transparent about it.
"My team works well and I'm afraid these changes will disrupt that."	Try to keep high-performing teams intact (what is working well).
"This will take forever."	Provide short-term milestones to help punctuate the change process with tangible endpoints along the way that can be celebrated.
"Nobody's asking me what I think."	Be accessible, approachable, and seek input to create ownership and commitment.
"Why would they start this now at the busiest time of our year?"	Carefully consider the timing of specific change actions and their impact.
"This'll lead to our best year ever? Yeah right."	Be realistic about projections, and don't oversell or over-commit.
"Can you believe how they told us about all this?" "Everyday somebody tells us something new about what we need to do."	Be sensitive to the emotional impact of communications about change. Customize and tailor communications to the emotional needs of those involved. Communicate through multiple methods and with honesty and integrity. Streamline communications. (For more on this, see Chapter 8)

indicate that not enough work has been done on sharing the rationale for change. Here's where some of the information we put together in Chapter 5 may be useful again. By referring to the business case for change that we have developed, we can help people understand the drivers behind a specific change. By sharing those worst-case and best-case scenarios, we can paint a vivid picture of the future for the people who currently aren't convinced of the need for change. We will find that helping people in our organization understand not only what change is occurring, but also why the change is occurring, is critical in helping people make the transition through the emotions of change.

Getting past personal "fear factors"

For other people, the reason they are less than enthusiastic about a change may have to do with personal fears about it. For instance, a director at One-Bank might state to the VP, "I've worked hard to get where I am in the company and this change is going to mess all of that up." If we dig a little deeper and have a conversation with this person to try to understand more about why she feels this way, we might find that the underlying reason for her negativity about the impending merger is a fear of losing power, a fear of losing status, and a fear of losing her job. Another employee might explain, "I've heard that this merger is going to mean a complete overhaul of our current systems." Probing this further, we may find that he has a fear of new technology and is afraid he won't have the skills needed to succeed in the new Two-Banks environment.

Someone else in our group might say something like, "The people I work with are my friends and my colleagues. We know each other well and work effectively together as a team." For this person, negativity about the merger might really be about a fear that the merger will disrupt personal relationships and team performance.

Working with people in our organization to uncover any underlying fears is imperative if we want to be able to alleviate those fears and help people make the transition to the future. Then, if possible, we should solicit ideas about how their fears might be overcome. For example, running a session on career paths at the post-merger Two-Banks to address the fear of a loss of status in the new organization might be helpful for those with fears about their careers. For those who are concerned about new technology, we might find out what type of training and development programs could be provided to help them improve their skills. For those worried about disruptions in personal relationships, we could explore whether there are some paths for retaining some continuity of working relationships – at least in the short run. If, however, the fact is that there is quite a bit of uncertainty about what is going to happen in a particular business unit, then the best we may be able to do is to demonstrate integrity by openly legitimizing their concerns and communicating where we are equally uncertain about the future.

Heads up
Where there's smoke – there's fire

Often many people share similar fears. Indeed, since emotions are often socially shaped, looking beyond individuals towards patterns in the emotional landscape of our organization may be beneficial. If we find that one person is afraid of a particular aspect of the change, then there are likely others who share this fear. That only one person has articulated his or her fear doesn't mean there aren't plenty of others in our organization feeling the same way.

Working through doubts about change agents

Another common reason that people experience negative emotions about a change is that they are concerned about who is leading the change. For example, at One-Bank, some people in the division might question the experience, character, or skill of the top management team that decided to move forward with the merger.

If concerns about the change agents involved seem to be at the root of people's negative emotions, there are a few approaches that can be helpful. If possible, we can work to establish and reinforce the credibility of the change agents. For instance, we could have them talk with the group and include a discussion of their credentials, past successes, and integrity. As well, we could work with them to ensure that their communications are transparent, honest, and straightforward. We might also explore the possibility that the change agents chosen aren't ideal, and consider adding others to the team to help bolster the skill set of the leadership team. Getting those who are concerned about the process more involved in what is happening is often a very useful approach, so we might even consider adding these folks to the team. These people will not only have the comfort of knowing their input will be considered, but will also move out of the role of being skeptics on the periphery towards being more positively involved with the change. Some executives may worry that pulling people onto the team as the change progresses may be perceived by others as an admittance of poor decision making of the initial composition of the team. However, the acknowledgement of other perspectives in a dramatic and emotionally charged change can actually reverse many of the negative emotions associated with senior management's actions, and lead to increased credibility and respect.

Respecting the history of change

Previous change experiences can have a dramatic impact on how people feel about the change they are currently facing. If people in our division at One-Bank have experienced a multitude of failed changes over the past year, they are more likely to be negative about the merger. If this is the case and the history of change is quite negative in our organization, it is important to help people consider the current change initiative on its own merits. We may need to disassociate this change from past change efforts, and underscore how the current change is different. Undoubtedly the content of the change will be different, but usually there are other differences as well. These might include the person who is leading the change, the approach to change that is being used, the timeframe of the change, the degree of transparency, and the criticality of the change.

If past changes have failed, we may also need to provide some tangible "wins" early on in the current change process. Most major strategic changes take time. By breaking down a change into smaller, more manageable components, we can create small wins, which build momentum for bigger successes down the road. Although strong proponents for a change may be willing to stay the course for long periods of time, most people need convincing proof that their efforts are paying off. Punctuating a large strategic change with a series of small wins lets people celebrate successes and see for themselves that results are being achieved and recognized. All of this builds further credibility for the change process.

If, on the other hand, recent change initiatives have gone well, we may want to point to these successes to help alleviate people's negativity about the present change process. We also may want to piggyback on those successes and draw parallels to those change initiatives whenever possible.

Heads up
Timing can be everything

The timing of any change can be critical. If a huge change initiative has just been undertaken and the organization is burned out on change, then the timing is probably not good to introduce another large change initiative. Similarly, if a particular time of year is hectic for our business, then we may want to explore whether there is flexibility to embark upon change initiatives during calmer periods.

Ahead of the curve
Start from what is working well

If the change we are embarking on is one that does springboard off from what is already working well, then let people know this. By underscoring that the future is actually about accentuating parts of the past, we can give people confidence that the future is not so uncertain, and indeed will capture the past. For example, perhaps a change we are pursuing now actually aligns perfectly with a well-respected founder of our company's original vision. Making those connections transparent to people in our organization may help them be more receptive to the changes we are proposing.

People's emotions may indicate a need to change the change

While emotions can often be worked through, we also want to leave open the possibility that the negative emotions being expressed by people in our organization are actually indicative of a problem with the change that is being pursued. For example, if people in our organization come up with well-articulated arguments against a change, and we know that these arguments have never been considered, we will definitely want to learn from these people rather than simply try to work with their emotions. In these instances, where people's reactions do in fact indicate that something important has been overlooked or needs to be rethought, we may need to go back to the drawing board in answering the question, "What changes do we need to make?" or "How are we going to implement these changes and build in dynamism?" In doing so, we may want to consider involving more people in our organization – especially those who have been particularly negative. Working with these people to come up with alternative recommended changes may not only lead to better decisions about what to do and how to do it, but may also lead to creating ownership and commitment from people who have previously been very negative. This, in turn, will result in a greater likelihood of sustainable success.

Key takeaways for Chapter 7

- Appreciate that everyone will react differently to a particular change, and that everyone travels through a personal emotional journey at his or her own pace.
- Try to understand how different people are feeling about a change, and validate their emotions.
- Keep communication channels open.
- Determine where folks need to be for change to be successful, rather than try to get everyone to "You betcha."
- Explore why people are experiencing negative emotions about a change. Common reasons include:
  - not understanding the change or the drivers for the change
  - fearing job loss, loss of status, or lack of skills
  - doubting the abilities and motives of the change agents
  - viewing the current change in light of past change failures
  - questioning whether the proposed change is sound.
- Once we understand why people feel the way they do, we need to explore action steps that will help support their transition to the future.
- How emotions are supported affects not only the success of this change but also receptivity to future changes.

Tools
Supporting emotional transitioning tool

Step 1: Note how each of our direct reports currently seem to be feeling about the change, using the continuum of "Not a chance" to "You betcha."

Step 2: Note where we think each of these individuals needs to be for change to be successful.

Individual	"Not a chance" ⟶ "Do we have to?" ⟶ "You betcha"
Bill	▲————————————————➤ ★

▲ = How an individual is currently feeling about the change

★ = Where we think they need to be for change to be successful

128

Step 3: Talk with each individual to figure out why they feel the way they do and explore possible action steps that might be taken to help them feel more positively about the change.

Name and role in change	Where s/he is now?	Why?	Where does s/he need to be for change to be successful?	Other relevant issues	Possible action steps to support emotional transitioning			
Bill Well-connected supervisor in the bank Key leader of various aspects of implementation	"Not a chance"	Fears it will disrupt his working relationships Not sure the change agent is a good choice Got moved in the last change	"You betcha"	His team loves working with him and his emotions affect others His 9 year old son has a number of ongoing health issues	Talk with him about who is important to work with and align him and those people See if others feel the same way about the folks leading the change Underscore how this change is different from the last and the benefits See if he needs some support or resources to help with his son			

8 Planning the implementation details

To ensure that any changes we embark upon move quickly and progress smoothly, it is essential for us to consider the details of "how" a change should transpire. Right from the start, we will want to strive to create strong ownership for implementation by involving people in the process. We will also want to identify and prioritize the core activities of our change initiative, and consider the timing and sequencing of these activities. Effective communication throughout the process is essential, and we will want to create feedback loops to capture ideas and adjust the implementation plan accordingly. These steps will lead to success in the current change, and create a positive platform for future change initiatives.

At the same time, the reality of change is that we cannot control every aspect of it, nor can we *always* be prepared for *everything*. Hiring a vice-president for the new division might take longer than expected, or the new equipment needed

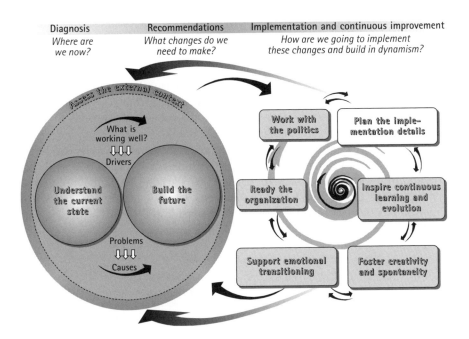

Figure 8.1 The SOC framework: planning the implementation details

in the plant might not arrive on time, or the announcement of two competitors merging might put a whole new spin on the change. So, while planning is essential, any number of things can transpire throughout change that we cannot anticipate. The key is having a plan in place that not only addresses the necessary details but also contains room for flexibility and dynamism. Although *how* we implement a change may not end up being exactly as originally envisioned, planning will increase our odds of being able to achieve success.

At a Glance
Planning the Implementation Details

- Who should be involved?
- Identifying the core activities
- Determining pace and timing
- Empowering others to specify relevant details
- Communicate, communicate, communicate
- Contingency planning for the bumps along the way

WHO SHOULD BE INVOLVED?

One of the first things we will want to think about when developing an implementation plan is who should be involved. A good place to start is by thinking about who will be impacted by the change, and who can help create a more powerful change platform and help mobilize ownership and commitment to the change. Typically top managers are included in planning processes, but it is critical to also include middle managers and frontline employees. Some people would rather hear about change or its details from people they know well than from those at the top. Often this might be someone who works in their unit rather than someone higher in the organization.

Beyond those people immediately obvious to us in various units and levels of our organization, we will also want to include key informal leaders in the organization. Referring back to Chapter 6, Working with the politics of change, may be helpful here. The insights we gained from our political analysis can help us identify those people outside the formal structure that may be very useful in mobilizing our change initiative.

Ahead of the curve
When to devote extra attention to planning the implementation details

Although planning the implementation details is critical in all change capable organizations, it is especially beneficial when:

- we know what we want to change and are looking for help on how to make it happen
- we know we need to create an implementation plan for a change we have got in the works but are not sure how to accomplish this task
- we have got a plan but want to ensure it is comprehensive enough to ensure a successful implementation
- we are in the midst of a change that is disorganized, creating lots of confusion, and is running behind schedule.

Heads up
Planning is not a one-time event

Planning is not something that we do at the outset of a change implementation and never return to again. As a change progresses, plans will need to adapt and evolve to ensure that they are still meaningful to our organization. With this in mind, we should revisit our implementation plan regularly to check progress and modify the plan if necessary.

The inclusion of external stakeholders is also valuable because organizational change never occurs in a vacuum. Customers, suppliers, government lobbyists, and local communities can all be impacted by organizational change. Including these groups when planning the details of change can offer important insights, minimize negative effects, and lead to greater coordination of implementation across stakeholders.

By involving folks from inside and outside the organization, we gain the knowledge needed to plan effectively and we also build people's commitment to the change process – not only for the current change initiative but also for the ongoing change that is inevitable in today's fast-paced business environments.

Heads up
Enlist others to determine key players

Some change leaders make the mistake of assuming that they can identify key players on their own. But enlisting the help of others in determining who should be involved is a good way of ensuring we don't miss key groups or individuals required for planning the details.

Ahead of the curve
Seek help from past change leaders

People that have been effective change leaders in the past often have tremendously valuable insights about how to deftly maneuver through change. They may be good people to include in the process because they often have a wealth of information about who to involve, frequently occurring stumbling blocks, and more efficient paths to success.

How much involvement is best?

Once the people who should be involved in the change initiative have been identified, we will want to think about the degree of involvement that's ideal given the specific changes being contemplated. Peter Senge et al., in their book *The Fifth Discipline Fieldbook* (1994), offer a useful tool that we have adapted, as shown in Figure 8.2.

Each form of involvement has its benefits and drawbacks. For example, while "telling" is extremely fast, it tends to result in less commitment and greater barriers to change. Also, telling provides no opportunity for the critical input that is often needed for change to be successful. With "selling," we often end up with compliance but the downside is that, again, we have missed the opportunity to gain input from those impacted by the change. "Testing" is better because we do receive some feedback. However, with

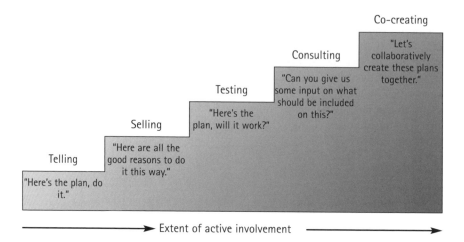

Figure 8.2 Degree of active involvement in change

Adapted from: Senge, P. (1994) *The Fifth Discipline Fieldbook*, New York: Currency Doubleday, pp. 314–28.

testing, we often do not obtain the full range of possibilities since ideas are already fairly developed before feedback is sought. "Consulting" moves us towards a scenario where commitment is more likely and input is gathered, but it takes time. "Co-creating" is the most ideal for helping folks get on board, but the downside is that, like consulting, it takes more time and also runs the risk of ideas being diluted and watered down.

While the optimal degree of involvement will depend on the specific change, a combination of testing, consulting, and co-creating is usually most effective. This approach enables us to obtain the commitment and input required for success in a timely fashion. Often, it makes sense to create a task force of key formal and informal stakeholders who co-create the change by consulting and testing the ideas and details through multiple communication channels with their units or divisions. In effect, a rippling and cascading process is created that enables us to get the reach and details right.

Consider a medium-sized consulting firm that is planning to roll out a new work–life balance initiative. Since this initiative is company-wide and everyone will ultimately be impacted by the change, involving key leaders from the various business units, whether they are formal heads of those units or informally powerful, as well as representatives from all levels of the company, would be important. An overall task force to oversee the entire initiative might also be a good idea. Also, task forces within each business unit might be helpful to address specific issues and to customize the initiative to their unit. However the task force is constructed, constant communication, feedback, input, and cascading out and across units and back is critical. This will help gain valuable input and prevent misunderstandings, redundancy, and wasted efforts.

Ahead of the curve
Train the trainer

In large organizations, a "train the trainer" approach can be helpful. This approach involves a core set of individuals who then train others to lead various phases or activities in the change initiative. The "train the trainer" approach can help ensure that various activities have a wide reach. In addition, folks may feel like they have more access and input into the change because they are working in smaller groups with trainers they are likely to already know.

IDENTIFYING THE CORE ACTIVITIES

Once we have identified who should be involved in the change and the degree of involvement, we can work on determining what the high-level core activities are likely to be for implementation.

Identifying the high-level core activities that need to take place for a change to be successful is a critical step in developing any implementation plan. Revisiting Chapter 4, "Building the future of our organization", can reveal many of these core activities such as changes in structure, leadership, rewards, HR practices, and physical layout. A valuable tool for organizing these core activities is a project-planning template that captures core activities, staffing, resources, deliverables, interdependencies, and timeframes for completion.

Consider the medium-sized consulting firm introduced earlier in this chapter that is planning to roll out a new work–life balance initiative. Initial high-level core activities might include several phases such as:

- conducting research on best practice work–life balance programs and initiatives both within and outside the industry
- developing a transition management team called the "Work–Life Balance Task Force" to lead and guide the initiative
- raising awareness about both the bottom-line and individual benefits of work–life balance
- building a communication plan to support the rollout of the work–life initiative
- creating metrics to evaluate the impact and success of the change
- institutionalizing work–life balance through changes to compensation, rewards, and performance appraisals
- developing ongoing input and feedback mechanisms for monitoring and modifying the change and gathering new ideas

As part of planning the core activities, it is always a good idea to see if the change we are implementing maps well onto other initiatives and strategic plans already underway in our company. For example, maybe the change our team is working on involves the implementation of new technology that will enhance customer delivery tracking. By incorporating this change under the larger umbrella of a company-wide push towards greater customer satisfaction and service, we may find synergies with other changes already underway. We may also discover useful insights from these other initiatives that will allow us to navigate more successfully through our change.

Some companies also find it valuable to create cultural icons, messages, and "advertising" to help keep folks mobilized for change. In essence, this means creating a "cultural wrap" to surround the change. For example, a manufacturing company might wrap its clean air initiative in the slogan "It's not only the business thing to do, it's the right thing to do!"

At one consumer goods company that was initiating a change around more transparency in communication and more openness and freedom of expression, "dead moose on the table" became the cultural symbol of this shift towards more "open speak" in meetings and decision making. The story is that some marketers were lost in the woods looking for a way home. They stumbled across a cabin in the woods and knocked on the door and were invited in. In the middle of the room was an enormous dead moose on the table, which none of them said anything about. They simply asked for their directions and left. In short, there was a dead moose in front of them and they didn't utter a word about it.

By using this "legend" of the dead moose, this company has created a cultural symbol that underscores the importance of speaking openly and candidly. So, whether the "cultural wrap" of a change is a dead moose or something else, it is often helpful as part of planning the details to consider whether there are symbols, stories, or icons that can be used to help build interest and momentum.

DETERMINING PACE AND TIMING

Once we know who is involved and the core activities, we need to figure out when we want to get started and the pace of the change. We will also want to determine the sequencing and timelines for the various milestones within the plan and our measurements for success. Some of the considerations in determining when to launch the change and the optimal pace include whether the necessary resources are available, the commitment level of people impacted by the change, the current financial situation of the company, as well as forces in the external business environment.

For example, if we return to the work–life balance initiative, the timeframe may be a bit ambiguous. On the one hand, it might make sense to move sooner rather than later if finding qualified people is challenging in the current job market or if the firm has been losing high performers due to difficulties juggling their career and personal life. On the other hand, moving too fast might mean some folks feel like the change is being forced on them with little opportunity to provide input or time to adjust. The key then is to work with those affected to set up a reasonable timeframe for our organization, given the change challenges we are tackling and the external forces behind our change. It is also wise to leave some room for the unexpected situations that will inevitably arise and extend the time needed to complete certain activities.

Heads up
Better to overestimate than underestimate time

When forecasting the amount of time a change will take, be realistic and get lots of input. It is better to be a bit cautious and deliver ahead of time than to overestimate how quickly things can happen and risk losing momentum and commitment. If there is a good track record for delivering successful initiatives on time, future change initiatives will have credibility from the get-go instead of being met with cynicism about whether the initiative will really get implemented on time.

Consider a pilot test

Another dimension of figuring out what needs to happen is to decide whether the whole change should be rolled out at one time or whether it makes sense to roll it out in a more phased approach. Rolling the whole change out at once is a better option when we want to implement several changes simultaneously throughout our organization or one change in conjunction with other change initiatives throughout our company. Similarly, if there is a fear that pilot initiatives might create resistance or resentment, or may result in a watered-down change initiative, then rolling out a whole change at once makes sense. Phasing in change with smaller pilot projects is a good idea when we want to test out or refine either the nature of the change or the means by which it is implemented. Pilots are also useful for demonstrating success, creating some quick wins, and building momentum.

For example, take the consulting company that is implementing the new work–life balance initiative. Rather than rolling the whole thing out to the entire company at once, there may be some groups within the company that seem to be more receptive than others. If this is the case, then it might make sense to use these receptive groups to start piloting specific changes such as the incorporation of work–life issues into performance appraisals. In this type of situation, holding off on working with less receptive groups until after some success and momentum has been built with the pilot initiatives can be a good idea. At the same time, it's important to be sensitive to how other groups might react (positively or negatively) if changes are begun in some groups but not others.

Setting and sequencing milestones

We will also want to think about setting and sequencing milestones. Usually, we will find that there are interdependencies between many of the core activities we identify for our implementation plan. While the sequencing of some of the activities and details will seem natural to us, it is important to think through all the sequencing and to set key milestones for achieving success in the end. Consider the following questions:

- In what sequence should the core activities occur?
- Are there interdependencies among the core activities that will impact this sequencing?
- Are some activities ready to roll and others not? How will this reality impact the sequencing of core activities?

For instance, with the work–life balance initiative example, recall some of the high-level core activities listed previously. Amongst these core activities, there is some natural sequencing that is obvious. For instance, raising awareness should definitely start before making changes to compensation, rewards, and performance appraisals. Similarly, developing a TMT communication plan and metrics early on in the change process would be critical. However, it is important to keep in mind that resource availability and organizational readiness may impact the sequencing of these core activities.

Ahead of the curve
Measure what matters

In every change it's important to develop measures to use as benchmarks for success. It's useful to have measures such as increased market share or profitability but it is often helpful to supplement those with more direct measures of the specific change as well. For example, if the changes implemented are supposed to yield improved product innovation, then the number of new product ideas, launches, or patents might be good measures. Or, in the case of the work–life balance initiative above, measures such as reduced number of sick days, lower turnover, less absenteeism, or even some creative indicators such as total number of miles walked or run by the organization, or improved fitness and health levels, might be appropriate.

Seek small wins along the way

In determining what is happening when, we will also want to consider the power of short-term wins. In an effort to speed the change process, too often only the long-run goals are emphasized. By breaking down what otherwise might seem like a neverending change process into smaller, achievable milestones, the opportunity for small wins is created. In the work–life balance initiative we have been discussing, the company could set an initial goal of reducing employee absenteeism by 5 percent within two months, or perhaps something more creative such as a goal of collectively losing 100 lb in one month. By communicating these types of incremental goals to people and, even more importantly, by communicating the *results* when the incremental goals are achieved, further awareness and momentum around the change initiative will be the result. Personal testimonials from employees talking candidly about the benefits of increased work–life balance on their job performance and healthy lifestyle could also be gathered and shared.

Ahead of the curve
Plan some activities that reinforce the change

Additional activities can also be developed to reinforce the new values

139

and mindset associated with a change. For example, the consulting firm we have been referencing throughout this chapter might hold a family picnic day that features not only healthy food but also a myriad of active games and sports for families to participate in together. Or, this firm might consider supporting a "bring your child to work day" or sponsoring a 5-kilometer walk/run for a good cause. Bolstering a change with a portfolio of activities that signal the new mindset often helps people settle into change more quickly.

EMPOWERING OTHERS TO SPECIFY RELEVANT DETAILS

Determining the key details related to each of the high-level core activities identified is another essential part of developing our implementation plan. Involving and empowering people in this process also makes sense, since for most changes, it is probably impossible for one person to singularly figure out all the key details that need to be addressed in order to achieve success. Consider using a cascading approach to gain input from people in various units and at different levels throughout our organization. For example, representatives from the TMT might function as the steering committee for a change initiative but might also approach people within their departments and functional groups to discuss the key details. By involving people beyond the TMT, the quality of information included in our implementation plan will be improved and the support for the change initiative will be broadened.

For example, the high-level core activity of "raising awareness" in the consulting firm might involve asking and working through the following key questions:

- What should this process of "raising awareness" look like for our organization?
- What key constituencies should we involve?
- What will be the key themes, messages, and ideas that will likely resonate for each group?
- What communication vehicles would be best for working with each group?
- How will we ensure that people's issues and ideas are heard and acted upon, and that their concerns are addressed?

COMMUNICATE, COMMUNICATE, COMMUNICATE

Communication is another critical component of successful change implementations. Effective communication ensures that the right people have the information they require when they need it. Often people think of communication as the means by which change leaders tell others what is going to happen. However, when done properly, communication allows for two-way dialogue and feedback to emerge. Potential problems and actual problems can be identified and addressed quickly rather than being left to fester. Spending time on planning for effective two-way communication is important because it cultivates commitment and ownership, creates transparency, demonstrates honesty, and reduces the likelihood that misunderstandings will arise. So, how do we go about effectively communicating with people in our organization? Guiding principles such as the following are key for designing effective communication approaches.

Use a variety of communication approaches ... but keep it manageable

If we want to be effective, relying on multiple communication channels is essential. Using a variety of approaches tends to be more effective than only relying on one or two methods. There is a wide range of possible communication tools to choose from, including the following:

- hot lines
- company town-hall meetings
- weekly area meetings
- one-on-one meetings
- task forces
- email
- posters/bulletin boards
- newsletters
- speeches
- websites/intranet sites
- online chat rooms
- idea boxes
- focus group sessions
- off-site meetings

All of these communication mechanisms can be helpful for different purposes and at different points in a change process. For example, if we want to impart factual information about a change implementation, a town-hall meeting combined with a follow-up email outlining the key details can be effective. For monitoring the change and assessing whether things are on track, focus group sessions and idea boxes can be ideal. To solicit ideas for improvement, we might consider using an off-site meeting, one-on-one meetings, or an intranet site.

In addition, decisions on which communication tools we use and how we use them will likely depend on whether we are seeking one-way or two-way communication and the level of interaction required. For example, finetuning the details of one phase of implementation might be more effective with a face-to-face meeting than with dozens of emails back and forth amongst key players. In addition, as we design our communication strategy, we should try to discern which communication modes are most effective for a particular message and audience. We may also want to try multiple modes for the same message, given that different people tune into different modes of communication in different ways. On the other hand, we don't want to use so many different approaches for the same message that people feel barraged and annoyed. Information overload can create numbness to all information and result in a situation where no messages are being read or heard.

Consider again the consulting company that is trying to implement a new work–life balance initiative. They might try the following combination of communication tools. They could create task forces to oversee and customize specific work–life programs within different divisions. A company-wide town-hall meeting could be used to launch the initiative. The company intranet site and bulletin boards could provide basic information on benefits, programs, and policies. Weekly area meetings could be established to monitor progress, address issues, and solicit feedback. A monthly newsletter could be developed to communicate upcoming events and celebrate successes. And, finally, gripe sessions could be held every Friday to air complaints and frustrations and search for solutions.

Be honest and direct

We should try to make the implementation planning transparent, and be as open as possible about what is happening and why. While we may sometimes need to frame information in a particular way, we need to be aware that if the people we are communicating with feel that there is insincerity or inconsistency, they will quickly learn to distrust the whole change process. Even though it may be bad news that needs to be delivered, being straightforward and direct is important. In the long run, this type of approach will lay the groundwork of trust and openness that is needed for our organization to become change-capable.

Create realistic expectations

Throughout any change implementation, it is important that we create realistic expectations. Being overly optimistic about the payoffs of change can be motivating for some people but may leave others disappointed, frustrated, and feeling misled. Being overly optimistic about a change process can also undermine credibility for future change initiatives. Therefore, it's important to temper optimistic projections with realistic portrayals of what is most likely to transpire.

Make sure we walk the talk

We want to make sure that our actions support our words. No matter how many newsletters and speeches occur, if we behave in ways that are contrary to what we communicate, we will quickly lose credibility and eventually lose people's commitment to the change process. For example, let's return to the work–life balance initiative we have been following throughout the chapter. If the partners of the consulting firm launch the initiative at a town hall meeting and then continue to put in 100-hour weeks, while demanding similar schedules from the junior people on their teams, they clearly are not walking the talk. These partners would send a much better message to the organization if, instead, they didn't email or call people on their team after hours and during the weekend, and if they started taking time during the workday to go for a jog, take a yoga class, or head to the gym.

Don't forget about our customers and other external stakeholders

It is easy to forget about our customers and other key external stakeholders throughout change implementation. However, most changes do end up impacting these groups either directly or indirectly, so keeping them in the loop is important. In the work–life balance example, customers and other contractors would need to know about new policies that might impact access to personnel so that they can adjust their expectations accordingly.

CONTINGENCY PLANNING FOR THE BUMPS ALONG THE WAY

With every change, our teams should engage in some contingency planning. We will most likely all agree that predicting the future is very difficult given the dynamism inherent in our industries. If we take the time to think about the unexpected events that could arise and how they might impact our plans, we will be better equipped to handle the unforeseen. One way to deal with this uncertainty is to conduct scenario planning exercises as part of contingency planning. Scenario planning involves members of key functional areas and levels working together to brainstorm a number of different futures or scenarios that could possibly result from change. Tactics for how to deal with each scenario are developed and catalogued for future reference should that particular scenario come to pass. By conducting such an exercise, key organizational members are better prepared for unanticipated occurrences because they have considered such a circumstance or something like it.

Given that there will always be unexpected things that happen along the way, in addition to scenario planning, creating support and backup plans to help people work through unforeseen challenges is another vital but often overlooked aspect of strategic change. Support might take the form of hotline numbers for crises, a few key "go-to" people, and an online facility for asking questions that has a 24-hour response time, as well as regular postings of "frequently asked questions." In addition, while we want people to expect bumps and hurdles on many fronts, we will also want to underscore that together, everyone can pull through them, and that we will do everything possible to work through the inevitable ups and downs.

Key takeaways for Chapter 8

- Planning is essential for the implementation of successful change but must be combined with a certain amount of flexibility to enable the plan to adapt and evolve.
- A critical element of planning is determining who should be involved (for example, key players, past change leaders, relevant internal and external stakeholders) and what their role will be within the change initiative. Involving people in the change process enables us to develop more comprehensive plans, and gain support and commitment both for the current change initiative and for future initiatives.
- Identifying the core activities that will comprise the implementation plan is another important aspect. When planning these core activities, consider developing "cultural symbols or icons" for the change and check whether the change aligns with other ongoing initiatives and strategic plans. _Ladder of Success_
- A next step is to determine pace and timing, and sequencing of the core activities. Using pilot tests helps develop and refine ideas and shows how to move forward. Building in small wins creates excitement and momentum.
- Effective communication throughout change is essential. Using multiple communication channels, encouraging two-way dialogue, and seeking feedback ensures everyone is reached and important input is gathered for ongoing adaptation. Being honest and direct, creating realistic expectations, and walking the talk demonstrates integrity and serves to minimize cynicism.
- Contingency planning helps to ensure that change still moves forward when unanticipated events arise.

Tools
Planning the implementation details tool

The level of detail within any implementation plan will depend on the nature, scope, and scale of the change initiative. This tool is meant to begin the process and to provide an overview of the implementation plan details.

High-level sketch

Step 1: Create a "high-level sketch" for this change process considering the categories below and others you want to add.

Who is involved and extent of involvement?	Core activities, milestones and metrics	When should things happen (timing and pace)?
_____	leadership training (level 1)	_____
_____	_____	_____
_____	_____	_____
_____	_____	_____
_____	_____	_____

Alignment with existing strategic initiatives	Communicate, communicate, communicate	Other? (for example, cultural symbols, reinforcing events)
_____	_____	Encounter
_____	_____	_____
_____	_____	_____
_____	_____	_____
_____	_____	_____

Contingency plans
_____
_____
_____
_____
_____
_____

Drill down

Step 2: Once the core activities have been identified, begin to drill down on the key tasks or deliverables associated with each of the core activities. The following template includes some of the key elements of many project plans. Depending on complexity, using one of the many project planning software tools might also be useful.

Key core activity: tasks/ deliverables	Start date	End date	Staffing and key resources	Other considerations/ interdependencies	Timeline (in days, weeks, months etc.)	Current status			

9 Fostering creativity and spontancity

Think of a marching band playing every note as scripted, versus a jazz ensemble that improvises. In the jazz ensemble, even though the basic structure and melody of the music may be determined in advance, the musicians take turns and give each other room to innovate, have some fun, and try new things. This helps the overall sound by filling in the spaces while allowing each soloist to stand out. The result is an innovative experience that is rich and full, delivered by musicians who are passionate about what they are doing. Often, the music created through this type of improvisation is better than ever imagined, and it would likely never have emerged if the musicians had tried to plan it in advance.

While in organizations we sometimes feel the need to control and plan everything surrounding a change initiative, there are many times when letting go – like an improvisational jazz ensemble – can actually be the best approach. Empowering the folks in our organization to run with a change can yield

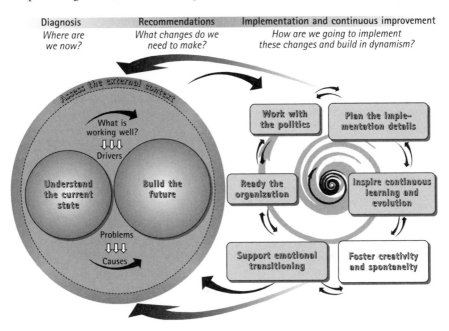

Figure 9.1 The SOC framework: fostering creativity and spontaneity

amazing results that could never have been planned in advance. As well, this approach tends to be inclusive and gives people within the organization respect and autonomy. This, in turn, breeds enthusiasm and commitment to change which enhances the likelihood that this and future change initiatives will take root and succeed. Although the focus in this chapter is primarily on how to cultivate creativity and spontaneity in a particular change initiative, nurturing this capability should be an ongoing process in our organizations.

At a Glance
Fostering Creativity and Spontaneity

- Sometimes planning is overrated
- Giving folks room to run with change can lead to amazing results
- Creativity takes time and requires incentives
- Creating the context for relationships to emerge
- Embrace rather than stifle conflict
- Maximizing input from the fringe yields creative insights
- Experiment with lots of small changes to discover bigger wins

SOMETIMES PLANNING IS OVERRATED

In Chapter 8, the focus was on planning, and certainly some planning and foresight is essential for successfully implementing change initiatives. However, sometimes planning is overrated, and we find that one of the tricks for cultivating successful strategic change is, at times, to actually let go. Organizations are complex and unpredictable, so planning and controlling every detail is virtually impossible. By the end of this chapter, we will realize that planning and controlling every detail is also unnecessary.

Ahead of the curve
When to devote extra attention to fostering creativity and spontaneity

Although fostering creativity and spontaneity is critical in all change-capable organizations, it is especially beneficial when:

- we are involved with a change and are seeking new ideas
- rapid and continuous change characterizes our organization, making planning difficult
- we are in an organization that tends to revert back to old ways of doing things rather than trying new things
- we are trying to implement change with a diverse range of constituents

- we are in the midst of implementing change and are having difficulties gaining commitment.

Ahead of the curve
What is complexity theory?

Much of the discussion in this chapter is based on thinking in complexity theory. Complexity theory draws from many different scientific disciplines such as biology, astronomy, and sociology. Some leading thinkers in complexity theory include Margaret Wheatley (*Leadership and the New Science*, 1999), Ralph Stacey (*Complexity and Creativity in Organizations*, 1996), and Richard Pascale *et al.* (*Surfing the Edge of Chaos*, 2000). The common underpinning is that the world is complex and comprised of dynamic systems. Complexity theorists believe that there are patterns in everything, even though at first blush things may appear chaotic. So complexity theories suggest that we, as leaders of organizational change, need to work with these complex systems underfoot towards our change goals. Furthermore, these theories suggest that we approach change in unconventional ways and recognize that the process might be different than we planned, and the outcome might be far greater than we even anticipated.

Ahead of the curve
We can let go for both the "What?" and the "How?" of change

Fostering creativity and spontaneity can be equally important in both determining what needs to be changed in our organization and figuring out how to implement a change. So, although this chapter is within the section of the book that strives to address implementation and the question, "How are we going to implement these changes and build in dynamism?", feel free to also use the information from this chapter in answering the question, "What changes do we need to make?"

GIVING FOLKS ROOM TO RUN WITH CHANGE CAN LEAD TO AMAZING RESULTS

Now let's start off by saying that "letting go" does not mean allowing things to spin out of control so that those people involved in a change initiative are heading in all sorts of different directions. Instead, "letting go" means thinking about how to align people within our organization towards a vision, and then letting folks cultivate that vision and figure out how it will be realized. It means providing minimum specifications and letting folks discover the best way to accomplish what needs to be done. As we get comfortable with letting go, we begin to realize that trusting in people's ability to self-organize and allowing approaches, ideas, and solutions to emerge naturally often leads to unexpectedly positive results. We find that creating a context that fosters creativity and spontaneity is sometimes the best approach our team can take.

Consider a progressive medium-sized chemical distribution company that instituted an employee stock ownership plan but was still struggling with chronic employee absenteeism. Some companies might react to this problem by instituting strict disciplinary measures in an effort to prevent missed deliveries and loss of customers. This company, however, chose to tackle the problem a different way.

Rather than assuming that those at the top knew best how to solve the problem, they empowered employees to develop a solution by giving them some background information about the problems that needed to be addressed. The process began by helping employees understand that the cumulative effect of individual absences led to disruption and constant fire-fighting in an effort to ensure that delivery schedules were still met. From there, employees were given full leeway in how to structure the work week for maximum individual flexibility within the constraints of the delivery schedules and work orders that needed to be completed. With ample room to run and unlimited possibilities, they developed a plan that not only solved the problem but was more innovative and effective than top management ever could have imagined. The employee-led solution let go of the need for tight controls. It assumed that it would be okay for people to choose their own schedules in a way that best accommodated their personal needs. Indeed, with minimum intervention and coordination by department shop stewards and a simple online "first-come, first-serve" scheduling program, the necessary daily and nightly coverage was achieved. Moreover, conflicts about scheduling dramatically decreased because folks were given the freedom to develop a solution on their own.

CREATIVITY TAKES TIME AND REQUIRES INCENTIVES

Creativity doesn't just happen in today's fast-paced, busy organizations; it needs to be fostered and nurtured. Employees need to believe that creativity and spontaneity are valued in order to devote time and attention to developing workable, innovative solutions, and we, as change leaders, are the ones that must walk that talk and convince folks that we are committed to exploring creative ideas. By dedicating time for creativity and providing incentives, we signal to employees that creativity is taken seriously and viewed as essential to being change capable.

There are many different ways we can carve out time and foster the creativity and spontaneity that can help us implement change successfully. While some approaches take quite a bit of time and effort, others can simply be folded in to the regular day-to-day operations of our organization. For instance, we could introduce weekly meetings devoted to creative thinking about either the implementation of specific change initiatives or the potential need for future change initiatives. This approach might consume as little as one or two hours per week, and has the potential to deliver high payoffs in terms of increased creativity. Or perhaps our organization could hold a special off-site meeting devoted to "out-of-the-box thinking" about a specific change initiative. This would require a one-time investment of anywhere from a half-day to several days, and might also prove useful in encouraging creativity and spontaneity. Or we might consider simply instituting an online employee suggestion program to help capture new, innovative approaches, solutions, and ideas. As long as we discuss the suggestions provided by employees, take action on those worth pursuing, and acknowledge people's contributions, this simple approach can also be highly effective.

In addition to allotting time for creativity, we also need to create reward and incentive systems that indicate the importance of creativity for ongoing change. These incentives might take the form of recognition for new ideas generated – the equivalent of an internal Nobel Prize. Bonuses for new ideas adopted are also quite common either through a one-time reward or as a percentage of profits generated by the idea. Another option is to create alternative career paths for creative individuals that allow them to continue to work on new ideas rather than climb traditional managerial career ladders. For example, many pharmaceutical companies have alternative career paths that lead to positions such as research fellows.

The reality is that, for the majority of us, creativity takes second fiddle to the day-to-day activities of our business. With all the meetings, emails, and firefighting that tend to consume our daily routine, there is little time left for creativity. Therefore, if we want to encourage new ideas and innovative thinking, we need to allot time and, more importantly, ensure that compensation and rewards reinforce those activities.

Ahead of the curve
Failing frequently is okay

Wayne Gretzky, a famous hockey player, once said, "I missed 100 percent of the shots I never took." The implication of his quote is that if we don't try things, we will never discover possible success. So, the trick is to ensure that folks in the organization know that failing frequently on different things is good because it means we are trying lots of possibilities, and some of those trials will pay off.

CREATING THE CONTEXT FOR RELATIONSHIPS TO EMERGE

In addition to allotting time and instilling incentives, we will find that another way to foster creativity and spontaneity within our organization is to create a context where the right people can be connected to form relationships that can be critical to a change initiative. By encouraging certain individuals to put their heads together, by bringing different functional groups of our organization together, or by forming a team from a diverse range of areas and levels within our organization, amazing ideas for change can often emerge. Consider a hospital emergency room where the average waiting time was 90 minutes, and during peak periods could easily exceed four to seven hours. This hospital was actively working to implement changes that would solve this problem. One approach that yielded great ideas on both what to change and how to implement the changes was to seed the right relationships. A task force of diverse stakeholders was put together that included doctors, nurses, receptionists, hospital administrators, and even recent patients who had been admitted to emergency. This group discovered creative solutions for minimizing duplication, streamlining procedures, and optimizing staffing levels that never would have surfaced if these constituents had worked on solving the problem individually. By connecting the right people, this hospital decreased waiting times significantly in a matter of months. In addition, since people throughout the organization were included in the change process, they felt ownership and commitment, which allowed the change to progress smoothly and quickly.

Thus, creating an environment in our organization where people with a broad range of perspectives and interests can meet and develop relationships is a great way to spark creative, innovative approaches, solutions, and ideas for making strategic change happen and enabling it to continue to evolve.

EMBRACE RATHER THAN STIFLE CONFLICT

Throughout the implementation of change initiatives, it is inevitable that people within our organization will have differing points of view, which sometimes can lead to conflict. People may have different interests, as was discussed in Chapter 6, "Working with the politics of change," or perhaps they have different feelings about the change, as was talked about in Chapter 7, "Transitioning through the emotions of change." Regardless of where people's differences stem, as change leaders, our natural tendency may be to want to reduce any conflicts that arise out of these differences. While extreme conflict can undermine the implementation of change, some tension and conflict can be good, leading to productive discussion and exploration.

Heads up
The value of informal relationships

If we find repeated conflict and deadlock between particular groups, one way to prevent this dynamic is to nurture informal relationships between these individuals. For example, if representatives from IT and logistics have developed an informal relationship through social functions, they may be less threatened by the other's suggestions, and will instead work hard to find a solution that satisfies both parties' needs. Now imagine informal relationships being developed across multiple groups that are involved in a given change initiative. Getting to know one another informally can be a powerful motivator to find solutions that benefit multiple groups and the organization as a whole.

Think about a team in our organization that always seems to hold an opinion that is counter to the popular view. While this team might be frustrating to work with at times, no doubt it also stirs up ideas and passion that otherwise would not emerge. This type of dynamic can lead to innovative and creative approaches, solutions, and ideas about both what needs to be changed and how a change should be implemented.

On the flipside, part of embracing conflict also means keeping a careful eye on tendencies towards homogeneity. While some homogeneity of views is good, because it suggests that folks are aligned towards common goals and prevents conflict from becoming pervasive, too much homogeneity can be detrimental to creativity. When there is virtually no conflict within our organization because there is so much homogeneity, the possibility of fostering creativity is low and the risk of groupthink, as discussed in Chapter 4, is high.

So while conflict can be uncomfortable and can seem less efficient than unanimity and continual cohesion, one of the keys to fostering creativity and spontaneity is making sure we allow for – and even encourage – conflicting viewpoints. This might mean that in meetings about a given change initiative, we candidly ask for differing opinions to be expressed or even go so far as to appoint a devil's advocate, whose role is to purposefully express contrary points of view. Or our team might intentionally bring together people or groups of people we know have different points of view. Regardless of the specific tactics we use, try to embrace conflict as a potential source of great ideas rather than as something that should be avoided.

Heads up
Push for actionable solutions to conflict

While cultivating conflict is critical for generating creative solutions, watch out for the "naysayer" who thrives on holding an opposing viewpoint but never takes the next step to offer ideas for solutions on how to address that viewpoint. Such behavior often originates from folks attempting to prove to the rest of the organization that the change is a bad idea. Sometimes a good tactic with these folks is to ask them to supplement their issues with potential solutions, or even have them lead part of the change. Increasing their involvement level in the change process often shifts their commitment.

MAXIMIZING INPUT FROM THE FRINGE YIELDS CREATIVE INSIGHTS

We can often find creative solutions and ideas in places where we least expect, so we need to keep an open mind as we approach change. One source of ideas that is often overlooked can be those folks who might be on either the "fringe" of our organization or on the "fringe" of a particular change. In the first instance, these folks might be those who "dance to the beat of their own drum" within our organization. These folks have non-traditional views that can be valuable in generating creative approaches, solutions, and ideas. In the second instance, these folks might be those who are indirectly impacted by a particular change, or perhaps even some people who aren't impacted at all but who might have unique perspectives to offer. For example, consider a Brazilian division of a large shipping company that is trying to implement improved workplace equality. A fringe source for new ideas on how to implement such a change may be the Canadian division cited as a leader in these practices for more than a decade. Tapping into the best practices of this division would likely yield creative insights that the Brazilian division may not have considered on its own.

Ahead of the curve
Positive outliers sometimes offer creative insights

Have you ever interacted with a department in your organization that you don't normally work with and been surprised to discover a new or interesting way of doing something that would be applicable in your own unit? Scanning for positive outliers such as this on a regular basis can often result in valuable ideas.

EXPERIMENT WITH LOTS OF SMALL CHANGES TO DISCOVER BIGGER WINS

Rather than seeking one grandiose change that will yield the desired results, another approach we can try is a range of different, smaller actions in different areas of the organization to see what happens. We can use these small tests as experiments for larger strategic changes. Or we may find that several small changes throughout the organization can be less costly and difficult to implement, and this can also yield excellent results.

Maybe there is a big problem in our organization, and since it is such a large problem, everyone's assumption is that a big change is needed to solve it. By considering the possibility that the size of the problem doesn't necessarily determine the size of the solution, creative alternatives for change can sometimes be discovered. There might be small changes that could have a big impact on solving a problem.

A case in point

For example, as Malcolm Gladwell discusses in his book, *The Tipping Point* (2000), New York City used to have a big problem with crime. Rather than one large change to the system, some small approaches were used to help solve this big problem. Specifically, graffiti was washed nightly from subway cars, people who committed the seemingly minor offence of jumping the subway turnstiles without paying the $1.25 fare were arrested, trash was picked up with great regularity, and police started walking the streets again instead of patrolling in cars. By implementing a number of small changes to the system, the problem of crime was significantly reduced.

In our organizations, there may also be small changes we could pursue that would have big impacts. Maybe a clever pricing strategy (buy three, get one free) might dramatically impact profits, or maybe we could save a pile of money if we improved the design of our product so it shipped more compactly and required less packaging. Regardless of the specifics, we shouldn't assume that a big problem always requires a big solution. Taking the time to look hard for small changes that might make a big difference is often very worthwhile.

Key takeaways for Chapter 9

- Let go and empower folks to run with change to fuel innovative ideas and build ownership and commitment.
- Allot time for creativity and underscore the importance of innovative ideas through incentives.
- Connect diverse people to spark ideas and creative solutions.
- Embrace conflict as a source of creativity rather than as something to be avoided.
- Tap into individuals on the "fringe" to gain valuable alternative viewpoints.
- Recognize that small things can sometimes make a big difference.

Tools
Fostering creativity and spontaneity tool

Step 1: Brainstorm ideas for how to foster creativity and spontaneity during the change process.

Run with min specs

Fail frequently

Tap into the fringe

Embrace conflict

Search for positive outliers

Allot time for creativity

Try lots of small actions in multiple places

Realize that small changes can have big impacts

Connect diverse people

10 Inspiring continuous learning and evolution

> It is change, continuing change, inevitable change that is the dominant factor in society today. No sensible decision can be made any longer without taking into account not only the world as it is, but the world as it will be.
>
> Isaac Asimov

As we have noted throughout this book, the external context in which most of our companies do business is fast-paced and unpredictable. For our organizations to achieve long-run success and sustain competitive advantage in this turbulent business environment, they need to be change-capable – not only adept at navigating the current change challenge, but also able to successfully change again and again and again.

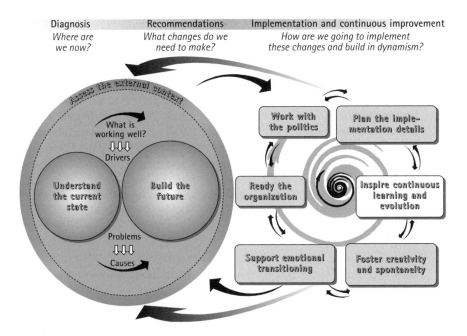

Figure 10.1 The SOC framework: inspiring continuous learning and evolution

161

In this chapter, we offer five overarching principles that change-capable organizations embrace to inspire the continuous learning and evolution required for ongoing change. While many organizations give lip service to these principles or engage in them somewhat haphazardly, change-capable organizations embed them in daily operations and activities. These principles include engaging in ongoing external sensing, utilizing stakeholder feedback loops, leveraging collective knowledge, creating a change-capable context, and nurturing change-capable thinking.

At a Glance
Inspiring Continuous Learning and Evolution

- Engage in ongoing external sensing
- Utilize stakeholder feedback loops
- Leverage collective knowledge
- Create a change capable context
- Nurture change-capable thinking

ENGAGE IN ONGOING EXTERNAL SENSING

As you may recall from Chapter 2, analyzing the external context is important for determining the types of changes our organization might pursue. Information about external dynamics also helps build commitment and urgency. In this chapter, we suggest that engaging in ongoing external sensing as part of the organization's daily activities provides the up-to-date, real-time information necessary for becoming change-capable. Incorporating external sensing into daily operations enables us to learn how to become experts at understanding and predicting the external forces that most powerfully impact our organizations. Beyond assessment, ongoing external sensing allows us to become proactive rather than reactive players in our competitive landscape. We are constantly attuned to macro trends, competitor moves and best practices, changes in customer preferences, and the interests of other external stakeholders. This allows us to "sense" change before it happens, and most importantly, to be aware of changes before our competition, creating a source of competitive advantage.

Ahead of the curve
When to devote extra attention to inspiring continuous learning and evolution

Although inspiring continuous learning and evolution is critical in all change-capable organizations, it is especially beneficial when:

- we find that we are always one step behind our competitors
- our organization copes with change fairly well but could benefit from strengthening its ability to continuously evolve and adapt
- our organization never seems to come up with the new ideas required to fuel the changes needed for long-term success
- we seem to have lots of good ideas percolating within our organization but we are unable to develop and take advantage of them
- people in our organization don't seem to have the knowledge they need when they need it, where they need it, and we don't do a very good job of gathering or sharing knowledge.

UTILIZE STAKEHOLDER FEEDBACK LOOPS

As noted throughout the book, stakeholder relationships and feedback loops are critical for building a change-capable organization. Whether those stakeholders are external or internal to the organization, continuously seeking input and feedback from employees, customers, suppliers, distributors, the community, and other groups enables us to gather the critical, just-in-time information needed for ongoing change. These external and internal feedback loops might take the form of quarterly focus group meetings, ongoing satisfaction surveys, or advisory boards that include key stakeholders. They may also include more informal approaches to feedback such as water-cooler chats, online chat rooms, lunch-and-learns, Friday afternoon happy hours, and company-wide town-hall meetings. Organizations that conduct such feedback initiatives on an ongoing basis develop the capability to know which stakeholders are most valuable for a given situation, how to design the most effective feedback loops for those stakeholder groups, and how to ensure stakeholder input is incorporated into organizational decision making. For example, maybe a leading robotics firm known for prosthetic limbs is struggling with how to make a more effective socket for the joint. Rather than simply approach doctors, it develops strong feedback loops with physiotherapists who are treating patients recovering from prosthetic limb surgery. This includes videotapes of patients discussing mobility challenges, as well as physiotherapists offering ideas for how to enhance movement. As a result of these strong relationships and detailed input, the robotics firm is able to keep one step ahead of their competitors on innovations in prosthetics.

LEVERAGE COLLECTIVE KNOWLEDGE

Engaging in external sensing and building stakeholder feedback loops are key processes for gathering the up-to-date knowledge needed for continuous learning. Equally important is having processes in place to ensure that the knowledge captured is shared and diffused appropriately. "Collective knowledge" refers to everything from skills and capabilities to information about strategic organizational processes such as decision making, product development, and technological innovation. Studies suggest that we only capture and record roughly 20 percent of the knowledge in our organizations. Yet being able to create, gather, organize, share, and diffuse knowledge throughout our organizations is a critical component of ensuring our organizations continue to learn and evolve. It ensures that people in our organizations have the knowledge they need, where they need it, and when they need it. This avoids wasting time "reinventing the wheel" and allows for the effective leveraging of knowledge for the benefit of customers and employees, and for the long-run evolution and sustainability of the organization.

Table 10.1 displays some knowledge management tools that leading organizations use to leverage their collective knowledge and optimize learning across the organization.

Many top consulting firms engage in knowledge harvesting by establishing call centers for answering consultant requests, databases for consultant skills, and FAQs. Some firms take knowledge harvesting a step further and create powerpacks, which are structured sets of online resources for people working in an area. A number of oil companies have found that they can save huge amounts of time and money by having folks in the field create on-demand, accessible solutions to common problems faced in the field. Some leading manufacturers use after action reviews as part of refining their new product introduction preps on their assembly lines. They run a new product on the line for a short period of time and then conduct an after action review to determine what went well with that product run, what needs improvement, and what to do differently the next time.

Regardless of the specific knowledge management tool used, leveraging collective knowledge becomes much easier with the advent of technology. Employees can upload and download key information from all over the world if effective knowledge management tools are in place.

Ahead of the curve
Common barriers faced in leveraging collective knowledge

In attempting to capture, share, and disseminate knowledge in our organization, we might hear the following:

"I don't have the time."
"I've got too much real work to do."
"That's not my job."
"I don't trust them."
"They're going to take the credit."

When we hear statements such as these, we may need to revisit and work through the "How?" of the SOC framework, treating leveraging collective knowledge as a change challenge. This would involve building commitment in our organization for the importance of these tools for ongoing learning and evolution as well as working through the politics at play, and the emotions involved in setting up better knowledge capture, sharing, and diffusion.

Table 10.1 Knowledge management tools

Knowledge tool	Description	Benefits
Knowledge audit	Overview of knowledge needs, resources, and flows within an organization.	Enables the organization to determine what knowledge it has, where it is located, who uses it, and for what.
Capturing and diffusing best practices	Organizational learning stemming from external best practices such as site visits, survey tools, and secondary research or the sharing of internal best practices such as operational efficiencies, innovations, or human resource management.	Avoids reinventing the wheel, minimizes rework, and saves costs.
Communities of practices	Voluntary, self-organizing networks of people (internal and external) who share an interest and who interact and learn together on an ongoing basis.	Encourages information sharing across diverse functions, levels, and divisions. Participants, scope, and purpose can easily evolve and change.
Knowledge harvesting	"Directories" of contacts for knowledge expertise in the organization that captures and documents the tacit knowledge and know-how of specialist experts and top performers.	Ensures that expert knowledge is disseminated throughout the organization through training manuals, databases, and direct contact with experts needed for a particular task or project.
After action reviews	Post-mortems of the good and bad of what happened, why it happened, what went well, what needs improvement, what lessons can be learned, and what could be done differently the next time.	Allows for documentation of key lessons learned and forces time for reflection – a critical aspect of learning.

CREATE A CHANGE-CAPABLE CONTEXT

Change-capable organizations tend to have some common practices that offer guidance for inspiring continuous learning and evolution. Although every organization will differ in the specifics of how it develops a change-capable context, some common practices include sharing leadership, embracing a long-term outlook, creating connectedness, streamlining bureaucracy and red tape, being positively predisposed towards change, reinforcing reward systems, encouraging ongoing training and development, and promoting work–life balance.

Share leadership

Change-capable organizations possess an energy level that is often missing in other organizations. This energy enables them to continuously embrace and work with the onslaught of changes they face. By sharing leadership, change-capable organizations create commitment and passion around the organization. This commitment and passion stems from giving people the opportunity to run with ideas, projects, or activities with minimal intervention. Leaders in change-capable organizations recognize that micromanagement and oppressive supervision create a climate of mistrust. Change-capable organizations ensure that people have the freedom, autonomy, challenge, empowerment, and resources to be creative, take responsibility, and achieve continuous success.

Embrace a long-term view

Shortsighted organizations tend to focus on this quarter's results or short-run stock price fluctuations with little regard for long-run consequences. Change-capable organizations flip this tendency, and instead focus on long-run results and sustainable success. This outlook permeates the organization in all aspects of operations, from responses to external trends and strategic objectives, to everyday decision making and the treatment of employees. A long-term view ensures that we look past the current change initiative towards creating the stream of changes needed for ongoing success.

Create connectedness

Creating connectedness across functional, product and geographic boundaries, as well as vertically in our organizations is key for knowledge diffusion, sharing leadership, sparking creativity, cultivating commitment, and continuous learning. As change leaders, we should strive to establish ongoing activities such as regular retreats, intranet databases, video-conferencing, key player job rotations (both functionally and geographically), and annual showcases of ideas, products, and best practices. The more we bridge and build relationships between different units and levels in our organizations, the more we learn from each other and provide our organizations with the fuel for ongoing adaptation and evolution.

Streamline bureaucracy and red tape

Generally speaking, the more bureaucracy and red tape that exist, the less drive there is towards continuous evolution. Endless layers of approval and slow, cumbersome decision-making processes discourage folks from pursuing good ideas, and in many ways can sap people of the energy needed for being change-capable. Therefore, if we want to inspire continuous learning and evolution, we need to simplify policies, procedures, and rules that inhibit good ideas from being heard and acted upon. Instead, we want to develop fast, responsive, streamlined approval processes to get ideas and change moving forward on a consistent and regular basis.

Recruit diverse people with a positive outlook toward change

To inspire continuous change and evolution, change-capable organizations adopt hiring practices that attract people who are excited by change and who offer diverse perspectives to the organization. These folks help create ongoing momentum for change, and provide the necessary skepticism for challenging traditional ways of thinking. So when new folks are hired, ease back on trying to make them "fit in", and instead try to value what they bring to the table that is unique. That uniqueness gives our organizations the out-of-the-box perspective needed for ongoing learning and evolution.

Ensure reward systems support continuous change

Reward systems have a dramatic impact on innovation and continuous evo-lution. If people are told that learning and change are important, but in practice they are penalized for engaging in behaviors and activities that help them learn and change, then it is likely they won't be too keen to try new things. If, however, people within our organizations are supported and rewarded for taking time to experiment, make mistakes, and learn, these behaviors will thrive. By promoting folks who demonstrate a willingness to continually change, learn, and evolve, we send a clear message about the importance of ongoing change in the organization. In addition, change-capable organizations often create incentives based on longer-term performance and measures that are broader than strict profitability.

Encourage ongoing training and development

Another way to demonstrate support for ongoing evolution in the organization is to allocate resources for learning and create opportunities for folks within the organization for training and development. Learning and development for a change-capable organization can range from bolstering business skills and techniques, and life skills such as time management, to white-water rafting in the wilderness, to simulate the unpredictability of the external context and the team's need for constant adaptation and learning. Change-capable organizations also try to encourage both internal and external programs. While in-house programs offer consistency in content delivery across participants, external courses and programs offer networking opportunities and alternative perspectives that keep things fresh for ongoing change in the organization.

Integrate work–life balance and wellness

Change-capable organizations ensure that they provide organizational support and resources that foster work–life balance and wellness. Studies have shown that most organizations underestimate the cost of employee stress, turnover, and poor morale that result from work–life conflict. With the advent of the Internet, email, and cell phones, where employees can be reached 24 hours a day, seven days a week, many of these issues have been exacerbated. Indeed, researchers estimate that work–life conflict costs organizations thousands of dollars annually, per employee.

Change-capable organizations, on the other hand, proactively address the issue of work–life balance by providing flex time, job sharing, compressed work weeks, subsidies and time for elder care and childcare, stress management workshops, maternity and paternity leaves, telecommuting, and encouraging the full use of vacation time. In addition, they recognize that they need to do more than simply offer these supporting programs and resources. Employees must be convinced that using these options will not carry negative stigma, and that instead, work–life balance and wellness will be viewed positively by the organization as part of good career management. These organizations recognize that downtime from work and the opportunity to pursue outside activities is essential. Strong work–life balance and wellness programs attract and retain the high-talent individuals whose commitment is critical for success. More importantly, they refuel and maintain the energy needed for constant change and evolution.

NURTURE CHANGE-CAPABLE THINKING

Thus far we have been talking about creating a change-capable context in the organization. Equally important is the development of a change-capable mindset. So what can we do to help create the change-capable thinking needed to inspire ongoing evolution and change? Some of the things that change-capable organizations find helpful include asking tough questions, looking at the world through multiple angles, being conscious of common cognitive traps, and accepting that change is inevitable and necessary for success.

Ask tough questions

In change-capable organizations, questions are asked all the time and tough questions are respected and encouraged. Whether in meetings, in the halls, or in retreats, asking tough questions is viewed as an essential element of the process of learning and evolution. Consciously or not, many of these change-capable organizations use a variety of Socratic questioning methods. These questions might include questions of clarification, questions that probe assumptions, questions that probe reasons and evidence, and questions about viewpoints or perspectives. The key differentiator between change-capable organizations and others is that asking questions within change-capable organizations is viewed as a source of competitive advantage that keeps the organization on its toes.

Look through multiple angles

Change-capable organizations also embrace the ability to look at decisions, actions, the external context, and even themselves through multiple angles. This means stepping into the shoes of others (our bosses, our peers, those who work for us and with us, our customers, our competitors, our primary stakeholders) and seeing issues from their point of view. Viewing from multiple angles enables the organization to constantly learn and evolve by thinking out of the box, avoiding groupthink, uncovering new insights, verifying assumptions and reasoning, and seeing issues from many different vantage points.

Be conscious of cognitive traps

In Chapter 4, we touched on self-imposed constraints and sunk costs as some of the traps that can hinder effective thinking and decision making when building the future. Change-capable organizations must be conscious of these traps, but should also be mindful of others that specifically hinder learning and evolution. These other traps include framing bias, recency, and generalizing from biased sampling.

Framing bias occurs when decisions are influenced by a particular point of reference that is then used to reach decisions that may or may not be optimal. For example, Nobel prize winner Daniel Kahneman and his long-time collaborator, Amos Tversky, well known for their research on bias in decision making (1974, 1984), have found that whether decisions are framed positively or negatively dramatically affects decision outcomes. When doctors were told that 200 out of 600 people would be saved with a particular medical approach, they supported it. However, when they were told that 400 people would die with the same approach, they didn't support taking action. Note that the ratio is exactly the same in the two scenarios; it is only the framing that differs. By

169

being conscious of how framing may bias our view, considering decisions from multiple angles, and involving diverse stakeholders, we can mitigate many of these types of effects.

The recency effect is a trap where we refer to what has happened to us recently as the basis for our decision making or reaction to an innovation or new idea, rather than evaluating the idea on its own merits. For example, if a big opportunity in Latin America has just bombed, we might be reluctant to enter with another product in the same region, despite facts suggesting that this product would have a fundamentally different result than the previous one.

Generalizing from biased sampling occurs when we take a limited or small sample or example as a depiction of predicting future events. This becomes a mind trap when it is used as a rationale for "This will never work here." Whether it is framing bias, the recency effect, or biased sampling, we see here the very powerful role these cognitive traps play in how open or closed we are to learning, new ideas, evolution, and change.

Accept that change is the norm

A fundamental premise in change-capable organizations is that change is the norm, and that sustainable success can only be achieved through ongoing change. Although historically, the idea of stability, equilibrium, and that "once change was 'over' things would get back to normal" dominated in many organizations, leading organizations today recognize that change is not an obstacle to overcome, but rather an enduring part of everyday organizational life that needs to be embraced.

Key takeaways for Chapter 10

- Continuous external sensing is necessary to keep our organizations attuned to ongoing changes in macro trends and competitors.
- Developing and utilizing comprehensive stakeholder feedback loops gives change-capable organizations the input and insight needed for continuous learning and evolution.
- Change-capable organizations recognize the value of capturing, sharing, and diffusing knowledge effectively throughout the organization.
- To build a change-capable context, we need to share leadership, adopt a long-term view, create connectedness, streamline processes, ensure that reward systems reinforce change, encourage ongoing training and development, and integrate work–life and wellness into our organizations.
- Asking tough questions, looking at issues through multiple angles, being conscious of cognitive traps, and accepting that change is the norm also nurture the development of change-capable thinking.

Tools
Inspiring continuous learning and evolution tool

Engage in external sensoring, utilize stakeholder feedback loops, and leverage collective knowledge

Step 1: How do we inspire continuous learning and evolution through external sensoring, stakeholder feedback loops, and knowledge management? Note in the appropriate columns what processes and practices are currently used, what processes/practices should be developed, key learnings, and implications of those learnings for action.

See table on page 173.

Create a change-capable context and nurture change-capable thinking

Step 2: How do we create a change capable context and nurture the change capable thinking that will inspire continuous learning and evolution? Note in the appropriate columns what processes and practices are currently used, what should be developed, key learnings, and implications of those learnings for action.

See table on page 174.

Inspiring continuous learning and evolution	What processes/ practices do we have?	What processes/ practices should we have?	What are we learning?	Implications for action
External sensoring • PEST(E) • competitive landscape • other industry best practices				
Stakeholder feedback loops • employees • customers • suppliers • distributors • government • local communities • etc.				
Capture, share, and diffuse collective knowledge • knowledge audits • capturing and diffusing best practices • communities of practice • knowledge harvesting • after-action reviews				

Inspiring continuous learning and evolution	What processes/ practices do we have?	What processes/ practices should we have?	What are we learning?	Implications for action
Change capable context • sharing leadership • long-term view • connectedness • streamlining bureaucracy and red tape • diversity and positive outlook • reward systems • training and development • work–life balance and wellness				
Change capable thinking • asking tough questions • looking through multiple angles • avoiding cognitive traps • accepting that change is the norm				

11 Taking action

You must be the change you wish to see in the world.

M. K. Gandhi

Never doubt that a small group of thoughtful, committed citizens can change the world. Indeed it is the only thing that ever has.

Margaret Mead

CHANGE-CAPABLE ORGANIZATIONS NOT ONLY SURVIVE ... THEY THRIVE

To win in today's fast-paced and complex business environment, we need to be change-capable – agile, innovative, nimble, and alert. Indeed, the ability to change again and again may be one of the most powerful sources of sustainable competitive advantage our organization can possess. Although the content of what we do will vary, the ability to successfully change is a core competence that we know will provide an enduring edge.

To build those change capabilities, we must become skilled change leaders who are able to excite, enroll, and energize those around us towards change. As change leaders, we need a hands-on, comprehensive approach that we can share across our organization. This approach must allow us to understand the complexity of the change challenges we face while, at the same time, provide us with a process that creates success not only for this change but for the inevitable changes yet to come. We need an approach that will enable us to overcome those bleak odds discussed in Chapter 1 and become one of the few organizations that succeed, again and again.

YOU HAVE GOT WHAT IT TAKES TO BEAT THE ODDS

Now that you have reached this last chapter, you have the framework and the tools you need to beat those odds. See Figure 11.1 for a complete version of the SOC framework with full detail. The SOC framework and the set of accompanying tools give you a user-friendly and comprehensive approach that change leaders throughout your organization can customize for any type of change or at any point along the change process. It enables you to address

175

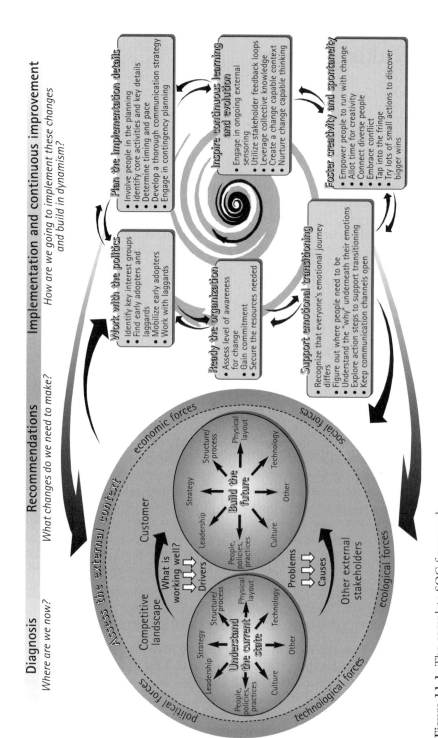

Figure 11.1 The complete SOC framework

Diagnosis
Where are we now?

Recommendations
What changes do we need to make?

Implementation and continuous improvement
How are we going to implement these changes and build in dynamism?

Plan the implementation details
• Involve people in the planning
• Identify core activities and key details
• Determine timing and pace
• Develop a thorough communication strategy
• Engage in contingency planning

Inspire continuous learning and evolution
• Engage in ongoing external sensoring
• Utilize stakeholder feedback loops
• Leverage collective knowledge
• Create a change capable context
• Nurture change capable thinking

Foster creativity and spontaneity
• Empower people to run with change
• Allot time for creativity
• Connect diverse people
• Embrace conflict
• Tap into the fringe
• Try lots of small actions to discover bigger wins

Work with the politics
• Identify key interest groups
• Find early adopters and laggards
• Mobilize early adopters
• Work with laggards

Ready the organization
• Assess level of awareness for change
• Gain commitment
• Secure the resources needed

Support emotional transitioning
• Recognize that everyone's emotional journey differs
• Figure out where people need to be
• Understand the "why" underneath their emotions
• Explore action steps to support transitioning
• Keep communication channels open

Assess the external context

economic forces

social forces

political forces

technological forces

ecological forces

Customer

Competitive landscape

Other external stakeholders

What is working well?

Drivers

Problems

Causes

Build the future
Strategy
Structure/process
Physical layout
Technology
Other
Culture
People, policies, practices
Leadership

Understand the current state
Strategy
Structure/process
Physical layout
Technology
Other
Culture
People, policies, practices
Leadership

the three essential questions of any change: "Where are we now?", "What changes do we need to make?", and "How are we going to implement these changes and build in dynamism?" More specifically, you are equipped to cover all aspects of change, including assessing the external context, understanding the current state, building the future, creating readiness, navigating the politics and emotions of change, working through the implementation details, fostering creativity and spontaneity, and inspiring continuous learning and evolution. So whether you are involved with large, transformational changes within your organization or smaller, more incremental improvements, you will be able to cultivate the change capabilities needed for both the current change initiatives you are involved with and those that are inevitably just around the corner.

START NOW!

So how can we find the time to use what we have learned, given that we probably have a desk full of priority items? Why not take 20 minutes right now and begin to develop an action plan for change within your organization? Better yet, see if you can grab as many members of your team as possible to collectively brainstorm future paths. Obviously, this action plan is not going to be complete or comprehensive. However, the idea is that by beginning to sketch out a change initiative, we will start to get the ball rolling.

One key change our organization should tackle soon

As you read this book, you probably thought of a number of changes that would be good for your organization to pursue sooner rather than later. Well, now is the time to focus in on one of those changes.

Where are we now?

Based on the thinking you did in Chapter 2, "Assessing the external context," and Chapter 3, "Understanding the current state," you have got a rough idea of where your organization is now. Jot down some of those insights in the "taking action tool" under step 1.

Based on that analysis, you also may have a number of ideas for a change that should be tackled.

Choose a change that will enable your organization to compete more effectively or overcome a significant problem. Or consider looking for things that are already working well in your organization, and use this opportunity to amplify or replicate this success across the organization. Note the change initiative you have chosen under step 1 in the "taking action tool."

Ahead of the curve
Choose change that matters

Many people in today's business world find that there is a schism between personal and organizational life. By choosing a change that is not only good for the organization but one that also positively contributes to the world beyond, we can bridge that chasm and simultaneously build more fulfilling professional lives of which we can be proud.

What should the future look like?

Chapter 4 discussed developing the future of our organizations. Given the change initiative you have chosen to embark upon, take a first stab at what the future should look like using the SOC wheel. In other words, what changes would need to be made in strategy; leadership; structure/process; physical layout; people, policies, and practices; technology; culture; or other dimensions of your organization? What metrics might you use to measure that success? Using the change initiative you have chosen to focus on, sketch what the future of your organization might look like along with the metrics to be used under step 2 of the "taking action tool."

How should this change be implemented?

In Chapters 5 through 10 of this book, many different dimensions of change were addressed. We walked through getting ready for change, working with the politics of change, supporting emotional transitioning, planning the details, fostering creativity and spontaneity, and inspiring continuous learning and evolution. Under step 3 of the "taking action tool," outline which aspects of implementation you think should be addressed first, and sketch out some key ideas under each, thinking about how they might be woven together as you implement your change initiative. In addition to sketching out the implementation plan for this change initiative, take a few minutes under step 4 to note ideas for inspiring continuous learning and evolution more broadly in your organization.

Getting going

So now you have a sketch of a change challenge you will take on and some ideas for what needs to be changed and how it might happen. Don't just leave these notes in this book. What will you do in the next week to get this going? What will you do by the end of the month to keep this on track? Return to the "taking action tool" and commit those ideas to paper in steps 5, 6, and 7.

CLOSING THOUGHTS

As change champions, we have the power to positively transform our organizations now and for the future. Whether we are in charge of change, nurturing change, or providing input, applying the tips, suggestions, and tools offered throughout this book will help build the long-run change capabilities our organizations need for ongoing success.

Key takeaways for the book

- Ensure that a comprehensive change approach is adopted by using the SOC framework (Chapter 1).
- Assess the external context to both justify why change is needed and provide insight on possible change solutions (Chapter 2).
- Understand the current state to determine what is working well and to uncover key problems and their causes (Chapter 3).
- Use the current state analysis combined with drivers of what is working well and causes of problems to build the future (Chapter 4).
- Get ready for change by ensuring folks are aware of the drivers of change, involving and engaging them in the process, and securing the necessary resources (Chapter 5).
- Work with the politics of change by tapping into early adopters' enthusiasm and helping laggards get on board (Chapter 6).
- Support individuals' smooth transition through change by validating their emotions and searching for action steps that will support their personal transitioning (Chapter 7).
- Involve folks in developing both the high-level plans and the specific details of implementation (Chapter 8).
- Leave room for the spontaneity and creativity that can yield surprisingly positive results (Chapter 9).
- Build in the dynamism that is essential for continuous learning and evolution by creating an organization that is energizing, fulfilling, and change-capable (Chapter 10).

Tools
Taking action tool

Where are we now?

Step 1: Jot down some useful insights about the external context and the current state. Use those insights to choose a change initiative to pursue:

Insights about the external context

Insights about the current state

Our change initiative

What changes should we make?

Step 2: What should the future look like?

SOC wheel: the future

Strategy

Leadership

Structure/process

People, policies,
and practices

Physical
layout

Culture

Technology

Other

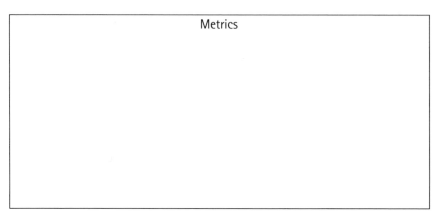

Metrics

How are we going to implement change and build in dynamism?

Step 3: Here is a sketch of the "How?" of implementation for this change initiative (e.g., some ideas for how to: ready the organization, work with the politics, support emotional transitioning, plan the details, foster creativity, and inspire continuous learning and evolution):

Ready the organization

Work with the politics of change

Support emotional transitioning

Plan the implementation details

Foster creativity and spontaneity

Continue to learn and evolve

Ongoing learning and evolution

Step 4: Beyond this change challenge, what else should we do to help our organization become more change capable? (e.g., better external sensing and stakeholder feedback loops, improved leveraging of our collective knowledge, building a change capable context and mindset)

Action plan

Step 5: Here's what we should do this week to get this started:

Step 6: Here's what we should do in the next month to keep this rolling:

Step 7: Other timeframes and milestones:

References

Barney, J. (1997) *Gaining and Sustaining Competitive Advantage*, New Jersey: Prentice Hall.

Dee, J. (2002) The myth of "18 to 34," *New York Times Magazine*, October 13, pp. 58–61.

Gladwell, M. (2000) *The Tipping Point: How Little Things Can Make a Big Difference*, New York: Little, Brown and Company.

Kahneman, D. and A. Tversky (1984) Choices, values and frames. *American Psychologist*, 39: pp. 341–50.

Kotter, J. P. (1995) Leading change: why transformation efforts fail, *Harvard Business Review*, 73(2): pp. 59–67.

Pascale, R., M. Millemann, and L. Gioja (2000) *Surfing the Edge of Chaos*, New York: Three Rivers Press.

Rogers, E. (1962) *Diffusion of Innovation*. New York: Free Press.

Senge, P., A. Kleiner, C. Roberts, R. Ross, and B. Smith (1994) *The Fifth Discipline Fieldbook*. New York: Currency Doubleday.

Stacey, R. (1996) *Complexity and Creativity in Organizations*. San Francisco: Berrett-Koehler.

Tversky, A. and D. Kahneman (1974) Judgment under uncertainty: heuristics and biases. *Science*, 185: pp. 1124–31.

Wheatley, M. (1999) *Leadership and the New Science: Discovering Order in a Chaotic World*. San Francisco: Berrett-Koehler.

Whitney, D. and A. Trosten-Bloom (2003) *The Power of Appreciative Inquiry: A Practical Guide to Positive Change*, San Francisco: Berrett-Koehler.

Index